A Choice of Bridges's Verse

A Choice of

BRIDGES'S VERSE

*Selected with
an introduction by
Lord David Cecil*

faber and faber
LONDON · BOSTON

First published in 1987
by Faber and Faber Limited
3 Queen Square London WC1N 3AU

Typeset by Goodfellow & Egan, Cambridge
Printed in Great Britain by
Redwood Burn Ltd
Trowbridge Wiltshire
All rights reserved

British Library Cataloguing in Publication Data

Bridges, Robert
A choice of Bridges's verse
I. Title II. Cecil, David
821'.8 PR4161.B6

ISBN 0-571-13844-6
ISBN 0-571-13845-4 Pbk

Contents

[vi]

[vii]

THE TESTAMENT OF BEAUTY

Introduction

(i)

Much admired half a century ago and by fastidious critics, the poetry of Robert Bridges is now neglected. Since he is one of the two or three authors writing in my lifetime whose works have meant the most to me, I hope that this selection will do something to rescue him from neglect. My aim has been less to try and assess Bridges's rank in the hierarchy of literature – always a futile sort of activity – than to show what I have enjoyed in his work and, if possible, to persuade my readers to enrich their lives by sharing in my enjoyment.

The poems of my choice are grouped under five headings: Personal Memories; Reflections on Life and Art; The English Scene; Love; and Miscellaneous, to which I have added a section containing excerpts from his long poem 'The Testament of Beauty'. I am aware that my arrangement may sometimes seem arbitrary and that some of the poems could be placed in more than one category. All the same I have kept to my plan as that best able to illustrate the individuality and variety of Bridges's achievement.

(ii)

The life of Robert Bridges, compared with that of most great poets, was remarkably untroubled. He was born in 1844 a member of the English country gentry, comfortably off if not rich, and the child of an intelligent and affectionate family. Gifted and good-looking, he was educated at Eton at a time when public school life seems to have been less strenuous and conformist than it became later; for, besides doing well in the orthodox roles of athlete and scholar, he found plenty of time for more unusual and characteristic activities. In the company of a few chosen friends, devoted to him and to each other, he cultivated a taste for literature and music, also for the study and practice of High Church Anglican religion; these last all the more enthusiastically because they were disapproved of by the more Philistine and old-fashioned of his schoolmasters.

This High Church phase passed when, in 1863, Bridges went up to Oxford; but he continued to interest himself in literature and music and to enjoy the society of his old friends. He also made some new ones, notably Gerard Manley Hopkins. Faced, after leaving Oxford, with a choice of profession a little surprisingly he chose medicine and practised as a doctor until 1881 when he retired for reasons of health. Three years later he married Monica Waterhouse; it was to prove an intensely happy marriage. Meanwhile he had settled down to dedicate the rest of his long life to literature. He was to publish a few prose works including some perceptive, beautifully-written memories of his friends Dolben and Dixon; but most of his productions were volumes of poems. These appeared at regular intervals and, though never widely popular, gradually earned him an honourable and growing reputation which culminated in 1913 with his appointment as Poet Laureate. The literary efforts of his later years were occupied largely with experiments in metre and diction. The effect of these showed in 'The Testament of Beauty', a philosophic poem which appeared in 1929 when he was eighty-five years old, to be more widely praised and read than anything he had written before. The same year he was awarded the Order of Merit, and the following year he died.

I got to know him in his last years when, already an admirer of his poems, I was introduced to him by Lady Ottoline Morrell. We got on well enough for him to ask me to come and see him. I accepted: it was to be the first of many memorable visits. His house, Chilswell, hidden by trees, was isolated at the end of a long lane on Boars Hill overlooking Oxford. This isolation was in tune with its social atmosphere which was eminently private and sequestered, but made welcoming to a visitor by Mrs Bridges's friendly courtesy, and vitalized by the personality of the poet, exhilarating, formidable, unforgettable.

I have met many other authors, one or two perhaps his literary equals, but none who impressed me as a man in the way that Bridges did. He was magnificently handsome in a style at once rugged and distinguished; tall and well-made with a white beard, thick wavy hair and splendid deep-set eyes. His talk was worthy of his appearance. It was not 'good talk' as the phrase is usually understood – it contained no eloquent discourses or polished quotable sentences – rather was it made up of casual spontaneous questions and comments and reflections, uttered in what has been well described as a sort of 'melodious growl', but animated by a Dr Johnson-like force and outspokenness and originality, often brightened by a bold, amused unexpectedness.

'I have been thinking lately about capital punishment,' he once said to me.

'Yes?' I replied tentatively, 'One does wonder if it is ever justified.'

'It is not that,' he replied impassively but with an ironic gleam in his eye. 'I was thinking that there was not nearly enough of it!'

He could surprise me in another way by asking my opinion about some subject – it might be spelling reform or how best to sing plain chant – in which he took an interest but of which

[3]

I knew nothing. It was one of the charms of his talk that he seemed to take for granted that one was his equal in mind and knowledge. This was gratifying though alarming to a youth nearly sixty years younger than him, and who regarded him with admiring awe. But it went along with what made his talk impressive as well as delightful; his attitude to the art of his choice and to himself as artist. Here it was that he was noticeably different from most writers I have met. All too often these have proved personally a disappointment; either because self-consciousness made them awkward and their talk commonplace or because they were afflicted with a streak of vanity which showed them too much open to flattery or over-sensitive to hostile criticism. Not so Bridges! Nothing could make him appear commonplace and he was far too independent-minded to be troubled by vanity. He did not overrate his work, as is shown by his readiness to ask and take advice about it from persons he trusted like Gerard Hopkins. But he was royally indifferent to criticism from others and appeared to take little interest in his public reputation. Indeed his attitude to his work stood out and has remained to me a model of what an artist's should be in that it combined an admirable self-confidence with an equally admirable lack of egotism.

His lack of egotism was encouraged by his view of poetry. This was unlike that of his contemporaries and more like that of the Elizabethans. Like them, he thought of poetry primarily as an art form rather than a means by which the poet could utter his mind and heart. He wrote of himself as a young man:

> What had led me to poetry was the inexhaustible satisfaction of form, the magic of speech, lying as it seemed to me in the masterly control of the material: it was an art which I hoped to learn . . . I did not suppose that the poet's

emotions were in any way better than mine, nor mine than another's.

The story of his later career indicates that he maintained this view for most of his life: he saw himself as a man who wrote less to express his personal thoughts and feelings than to put into the best words possible, thoughts and feelings which, for all he knew, were shared by others and in any case were no more valuable than theirs. For this reason he interested himself much in questions of poetic technique, and also turned his hand to many types of poetry – lyric, narrative, dramatic – mainly it seems to see what he could make of them.

The result was not always a success. Bridges's overriding concern with the formal aspect of poetry could lead him astray; for it left him seemingly unaware that a living work of art has a double character, that it must be at the same time an essay in a particular art form and an expression of the artist's personality. Much of Bridges's work, notably his dramas and masques, are in the main literary exercises uninspired apparently by personal thought or feeling. In consequence though accomplished pieces of writing they are without much artistic life. Luckily this is not true of his short poems: odes, elegies, songs. It is by these that Bridges lives as a poet. For, whether or not he intended it to be so, they are alive with a strong individuality that stamps them as written by him and by no one else.

This shows in his choice of subject. A large proportion of his best poems are inspired either by love or by the beauties of nature. Moreover these two subjects are often associated with each other by the fact that the poet sees both as related to what can be loosely described as his philosophy of life. This rested on his belief that man in his highest moments is aware of an ideal spiritual reality with which he longs to identify

[5]

himself. In the physical world we live in, this ideal reality incarnates itself as beauty. For Bridges this meant the beauty of the natural world or the beauty of the loved one. This is what drew him to these subjects and fired him to write poems about them. Further, his wholehearted unfailing response to the beautiful imbued his work with a pervading, distinctive sentiment. Its keynote is serenity. Not an unqualified serenity; Bridges was too thoughtful and too sensitive to be unaware of human suffering, let alone indifferent to it. His poignant verses on page 37 about the death of his brother-in-law, Maurice Waterhouse, show him capable of feeling deep grief, but, it may be noted, this does not lead him to cry out in protest against misfortune. For him, sorrow was something to be faced and accepted; sometimes without hope, never with bitterness. Consequently even his sad poems retain a sort of minor-key serenity.

His sad poems however are few. Most are happy and with a happiness confidently pitched in a major key. His love poems celebrate a fulfilled love; those describing landscape, even when it is clouded or wintry, are unshadowed by despondency. Bridges, in the words of Walter de la Mare, 'is the poet of happiness – not of mirth, gaiety, joviality, Bacchic abandon, but that of a mood, or, rather, a state of being, in which mind and heart are one, a balance between joy and solemnity such as delight and solace us in the music of Handel . . .' It is this Handelian quality which makes the pleasure given by Bridges's poetry so satisfying and enduring: for he had the skill to communicate it to the reader.

Indeed it was in his command of his instrument that his genius as a poet most fully and unmistakably reveals itself. It had always been the aspect of his work that had meant most to him. Did he not say that he had been led to poetry by 'the inexhaustible satisfaction of form, the magic of speech,

[6]

lying . . . in the masterly control of the material', adding that it was an art he hoped to learn. His hopes were fulfilled. He acquired complete control of his material and at his best achieves the 'magic of speech' in a fashion all his own. Unobtrusively but exquisitely it manifests itself alike in his diction and his metres. The first lines of 'London Snow' are an example:

> When men were all asleep the snow came flying,
> In large white flakes falling on the city brown,
> Stealthily and perpetually settling and loosely lying,
>   Hushing the latest traffic of the drowsy town;
> Deadening, muffling, stifling its murmurs failing;
> Lazily and incessantly floating down and down:
>   Silently sifting and veiling road, roof and railing;
> Hiding difference, making unevenness even,
> Into angles and crevices softly drifting and sailing.
>   All night it fell, and when full inches seven
> It lay in the depth of its uncompacted lightness,
> The clouds blew off from a high and frosty heaven;
>   And all woke earlier for the unaccustomed brightness
> Of the winter dawning, the strange unheavenly glare:

From 'London Snow'

Bridges's language here is unfailingly clear and precise. It also shows him subtly and imaginatively sensitive to the flavour and overtones of each particular word. This is especially evident in his epithets: 'high and frosty heaven', 'strange unheavenly glare', or, from other poems, 'O bold majestic downs, smooth, fair and lonely', or the 'soft unchristen'd smile' of Eros god of love.

The effect of the lines from 'London Snow' depends as much on the sound as on the picture. The movement of the

[7]

metre, in itself delicately melodious, wonderfully echoes the movement of the falling snow. Bridges's feeling for rhythm was at least as strong as for phrase. Now and again it seems to have been even stronger. In some brief lyrics – here he is very like an Elizabethan songwriter – he appears to be making use of the conventional images and phrases of traditional songs to give a verbal form to what is primarily a musical impulse: he wanted to compose a tune in words as a musician composes a tune in notes. The resulting effect however is not conventional or derivative for it is the tune that matters; and the tune is the expression of a fresh creative inspiration. Yeats, his great contemporary, says of these poems that they are composed of 'words, often commonplace, made unforgettable by some trick of speeding and slowing . . . every metaphor, every thought a commonplace, emptiness everywhere, the whole magnificent'.

True enough: but at his very best – in 'Nightingales' for instance, or 'Angel spirits of sleep' or 'The Voice of Nature', Bridges's work can be praised without paradoxical references to 'emptiness' and 'commonplace' for in them he has been inspired by his theme as well as by his feeling for form. Like the different notes in a musical chord, the two are fused together to become a single whole in which is concentrated the very essence of lyrical beauty.

Personal Memories

Elegy

Clear and gentle stream!
Known and loved so long,
That hast heard the song
And the idle dream
Of my boyish day;
While I once again
Down thy margin stray,
In the selfsame strain
Still my voice is spent,
With my old lament
And my idle dream,
Clear and gentle stream!

Where my old seat was
Here again I sit,
Where the long boughs knit
Over stream and grass
A translucent eaves:
Where back eddies play
Shipwreck with the leaves,
And the proud swans stray,
Sailing one by one
Out of stream and sun,
And the fish lie cool
In their chosen pool.

Many an afternoon
Of the summer day
Dreaming here I lay;
And I know how soon,
Idly at its hour,
First the deep bell hums
From the minster tower,
And then evening comes,
Creeping up the glade,
With her lengthening shade,
And the tardy boon
Of her brightening moon.

Clear and gentle stream!
Ere again I go
Where thou dost not flow,
Well does it beseem
Thee to hear again
Once my youthful song,
That familiar strain
Silent now so long:
Be as I content
With my old lament
And my idle dream,
Clear and gentle stream.

'The snow lies sprinkled on the beach'

The snow lies sprinkled on the beach,
And whitens all the marshy lea:
The sad gulls wail adown the gale,
The day is dark and black the sea.
   Shorn of their crests the blighted waves
With driven foam the offing fleck:
The ebb is low and barely laves
The red rust of the giant wreck.

On such a stony, breaking beach
My childhood chanced and chose to be:
'Twas here I played, and musing made
My friend the melancholy sea.
   He from his dim enchanted caves
With shuddering roar and onrush wild
Fell down in sacrificial waves
At feet of his exulting child.

Unto a spirit too light for fear
His wrath was mirth, his wail was glee:–
My heart is now too fixed to bow
Tho' all his tempests howl at me:
   For to the gain life's summer saves,
My solemn joy's increasing store,
The tossing of his mournful waves
Makes sweetest music evermore.

Kate's Mother

Perch'd on the upland wheatfields beyond the village end
a red-brick Windmill stood with black bonnet of wood
that trimm'd the whirling cross of its great arms around
upon the wind, pumping up water night and day
from the deep Kentish chalk to feed a little town
where miniatured afar it huddled on the coast
its glistening roofs and thrust its short pier in the sea.
  Erewhile beside the Mill I had often come and gazed
across the golden cornland to the purple main
and distant town, so distant that I could not hear
the barrack bugles but might spy the castle-flag
a speck of bunting held against the foam-fleck'd waves:
and luggers in black rank on the high shingle-bank
drawn up beside the tarr'd huts of the fishermen
(those channel boatmen famous for courage and skill)
and ships that in the offing their scatter'd courses fetch'd
with sunlit sails, or bare-masted outrode the tide:
'Twas such a scene of bright perspective and brave hues
as no painter can forge, brushing his greys and blues,
his madder, vermilion, chrome and ultramarine,
'Twas very England herself as I grew to love her
– as any manchild loveth looking on beauty –
England in the peace and delight of her glory,
beneath the summer sun in the wild-roving wind
the mighty fans hurtling steadily above me as there
Nature flooded my heart in unseizable dream:
  Long ago – when as yet the house where I was born
was the only home I knew and I no bigger then
than a mastiff-dog may be, and little of clothing wore
but shirts and trews and shoes and holland pinafore:

then was my father's garden a fairy realm of tree-
worship, mimic warfare and ritual savagery
and past its gates a land of peril and venture lay
my field of romance the steep beach of the wild sea
whither might I go wander on high-days for long hours
tended at every step by a saint, a nurse and mate
of such loving devotion patience and full trust
that of all Catharines she hath been my only Kate.

But inland past the Windmill lay a country unknown,
so that upon the day when I was grown so strong
(to my great pride 'twas told) that I might walk with Kate
on her half-holiday's accustomed pilgrimage
to see her old mother who lived across the downs
in the next combe, it happ'd that I so stirred must be
that after seventy years I can revive the day.

A blazing afternoon in splendor of mid-July
Kate and my elder sister and I trudged down the street
past village pond and church, and up the winding lane
came out beside the windmill on the high cornland
where my new world began. A wheel-worn sunken track
parted the tilth, deep rugged ruts patch'd here and there
with broken flints raked in from strewage of the ground,
baked clay fissured by drought, as splinter'd rock unkind
to a child's tread, and on either hand the full-grown corn
rose up a wall above me, where no breeze might come
nor any more sight thence of the undulating sweep
of the yellow acres nor of the blue main below.

For difficulty and roughness and scorch of the way
then a great Bible-thought came on me: I was going
like the Israelites of old in the desert of Sin,
where forty years long they journey'd in punishment:
'twas such a treeless plain as this whereon they went,
this torrid afternoon under the fiery sun

might be the forty years; but I forgat them soon
picking my way to run on the low skirting banks
that shelved the fields, anon foraging mid the ranks
fending the spikey awns off from my cheeks and eyes
wherever I might espy the larger flowers, and pull'd
blue Cockle and scarlet Poppy and yellow Marigold
whose idle blazonry persists to decorate
the mantle of green and gold which man toileth to weave
for his old grandmother Earth: – with such posies in hand
we ran bragging to Kate who plodded on the track
and now with skilful words beguiled us in her train
warning how far off yet the promised land, and how
journey so great required our full strength husbanded
for the return: 'twere wise to-day to prove our strength
and walk like men. Whereat we wished most to be wise
and keeping near beside her heeded closely our steps
so that our thoughts now wander'd no more from the way
(O how interminable to me seem'd that way!)
till it fell sloping downwards and we saw the green
of great elms that uplifted their heads in the combe:
when for joy of the shade racing ahead we sat
till Kate again came up with us and led us on
by shelter'd nooks where among apple and cherry trees
many a straw-thatcht cottage nestled back from the road.
A warp'd wicket hidden in a flowery Privet-hedge
admitted to her mother's along a pebbled path
between two little squares of crowded garden framed
in high clipt Box, that blent its faint pervading scent
with fragrant Black-currant, gay Sweet-William and Mint,
and white Jasmin that hung drooping over the door.
A bobbin sprang the latch and following Kate we stood
in shade of a low room with one small window, and there
facing the meagre light of its lace-curtain'd panes

a bland silver-hair'd dame clad in a cotton frock
sat in a rocking-chair by an open hearth, whereon
a few wood embers smouldering kept a kettle at steam.
She did not rise, but speaking with soft courtesy
and full respectful pride of her daughter's charges
gave us kind welcome, bade us sit and be rested
while Kate prepared the tea. Many strange things the while
allured me: a lofty clock with loud insistent tick
beguiled the solemn moments as it doled them out
picturing upon its face a full-rigg'd ship that rocked
tossing behind an unmoved billow to and fro:
beside it a huge batter'd copper warming-pan
with burnish'd bowl fit for Goliath's giant spoon,
and crockery whimsies ranged on the high mantel-shelf:
'twas a storeroom of wonders, but my eyes returned
still to the old dame, she was the greatest wonder of all,
the wrinkles innumerable of her sallow skin
her thin voice and the trembling of her patient face
as there she swayed incessantly on her rocking-chair
like the ship in the clock: she had sprung into my ken
wholly to enthrall me, a fresh nucleus of life-surprise
such as I knew must hold mystery and could reveal:
for I had observed strange movement of her cotton skirt
and as she sat with one knee across the other, I saw
how her right foot in the air was all a-tremble and jerked
in little restless kicks: so when we sat to feast
about the table spredd with tea and cottage cakes
whenever her eye was off me I watched her furtively
to make myself assured of all the manner and truth
of this new thing, and ere we were sent out to play
(that so Kate might awhile chat with her mother alone)
I knew the SHAKING PALSY. What follow'd is lost,
how I chew'd mint-leaves waiting there in the garden

is my latest remembrance of that July day,
all after is blank, the time like a yesterday's loaf
is sliced as with a knife, or like as where the sea
in some diluvian rage swallowing a part of the earth
left a sheer cliff where erst the unbroken height ran on,
and by the rupture has built a landmark seen afar
– as 'tis at the South Foreland or St Margaret's bay –
so memory being broken may stand out more clearly
as that day's happenings live so freshly by me, and most
the old widow with her great courtesy and affliction:
and I love to remember it was to her I made
the first visit of compliment that ever I paid.

Elegy

THE SUMMER-HOUSE ON THE MOUND

How well my eyes remember the dim path!
My homing heart no happier playground hath.
I need not close my lids but it appears
Through the bewilderment of forty years
To tempt my feet, my childish feet, between
Its leafy walls, beneath its arching green;
Fairer than dream of sleep, than Hope more fair
Leading to dreamless sleep her sister Care.

There grew two fellow limes, two rising trees,
Shadowing the lawn, the summer haunt of bees,
Whose stems, engraved with many a russet scar
From the spear-hurlings of our mimic war,
Pillar'd the portico to that wide walk,
A mossy terrace of the native chalk
Fashion'd, that led thro' the dark shades around
Straight to the wooden temple on the mound.
There live the memories of my early days,
There still with childish heart my spirit plays;
Yea, terror-stricken by the fiend despair
When she hath fled me, I have found her there;
And there 'tis ever noon, and glad suns bring
Alternate days of summer and of spring,
With childish thought, and childish faces bright,
And all unknown save but the hour's delight.

High on the mound the ivied arbour stood,
A dome of straw upheld on rustic wood:
Hidden in fern the steps of the ascent,
Whereby unto the southern front we went,
And from the dark plantation climbing free,
Over a valley look'd out on the sea.
   That sea is ever bright and blue, the sky
Serene and blue, and ever white ships lie
High on the horizon steadfast in full sail,
Or nearer in the roads pass within hail
Of naked brigs and barques that windbound ride
At their taut cables heading to the tide.

   There many an hour I have sat to watch; nay, now
The brazen disk is cold against my brow,
And in my sight a circle of the sea
Enlarged to swiftness, where the salt waves flee,
And ships in stately motion pass so near
That what I see is speaking to my ear:
I hear the waves dash and the tackle strain,
The canvas flap, the rattle of the chain
That runs out thro' the hawse, the clank of the winch
Winding the rusty cable inch by inch,
Till half I wonder if they have no care,
Those sailors, that my glass is brought to bear
On all their doings, if I vex them not
On every petty task of their rough lot
Prying and spying, searching every craft
From painted truck to gunnel, fore and aft, –
Thro' idle Sundays as I have watch'd them lean
Long hours upon the rail, or neath its screen
Prone on the deck to lie outstretch'd at length,
Sunk in renewal of their wearied strength.

But what a feast of joy to me, if some
Fast-sailing frigate to the Channel come
Back'd here her topsail, or brought gently up
Let from her bow the splashing anchor drop,
By faint contrary wind stay'd in her cruise,
The *Phaethon* or dancing *Arethuse*,
Or some immense three-decker of the line,
Romantic as the tale of Troy divine;
Ere yet our iron age had doom'd to fall
The towering freeboard of the wooden wall,
And for the engines of a mightier Mars
Clipp'd their wide wings, and dock'd their soaring spars.
The gale that in their tackle sang, the wave
That neath their gilded galleries dasht so brave
Lost then their merriment, nor look to play
With the heavy-hearted monsters of to-day.

   One noon in March upon that anchoring ground
Came Napier's fleet unto the Baltic bound:
Cloudless the sky and calm and blue the sea,
As round Saint Margaret's cliff mysteriously,
Those murderous queens walking in Sabbath sleep
Glided in line upon the windless deep:
For in those days was first seen low and black
Beside the full-rigg'd mast the strange smoke-stack,
And neath their stern revolv'd the twisted fan.
Many I knew as soon as I might scan,
The heavy *Royal George*, the *Acre* bright,
The *Hogue* and *Ajax*, and could name aright
Others that I remember now no more;
But chief, her blue flag flying at the fore,
With fighting guns a hundred thirty and one,
The Admiral ship *The Duke of Wellington*,

Whereon sail'd George, who in her gig had flown
The silken ensign by our sisters sewn.
The iron Duke himself, – whose soldier fame
To England's proudest ship had given her name,
And whose white hairs in this my earliest scene
Had scarce more honour'd than accustom'd been, –
Was two years since to his last haven past:
I had seen his castle-flag to fall half-mast
One morn as I sat looking on the sea,
When thus all England's grief came first to me,
Who hold my childhood favour'd that I knew
So well the face that won at Waterloo.

But now 'tis other wars, and other men; –
The year that Napier sail'd, my years were ten –
Yea, and new homes and loves my heart hath found:
A priest has there usurped the ivied mound,
The bell that call'd to horse calls now to prayers,
And silent nuns tread the familiar stairs.
Within the peach-clad walls that old outlaw,
The Roman wolf, scratches with privy paw.

ECLOGUE III

Fourth of June at Eton

RICHARD AND GODFREY

RICHARD

Beneath the wattled bank the eddies swarm
In wandering dimples o'er the shady pool:
The same their chase as when I was at school;
The same the music, where in shallows warm
The current, sunder'd by the bushy isles,
Returns to join the main, and struggles free
Above the willows, gurgling thro' the piles:
Nothing is changed, and yet how changed are we!
– What can bring Godfrey to the Muses' bower?

GODFREY

What but brings you? The festal day of the year;
To live in boyish memories for an hour;
See and be seen: tho' you come seldom here.

RICHARD

Dread of the pang it was, fear to behold
What once was all myself, that kept me away.

GODFREY

You miss new pleasures coveting the old.

RICHARD

They need have prudence, who in courage lack;
'Twas that I might go on I looked not back.

GODFREY

Of all our company he, who, we say,
Fruited the laughing flower of liberty!

RICHARD

Ah! had I my desire, so should it be.

GODFREY

Nay, but I know this melancholy mood;
'Twas your poetic fancy when a boy.

RICHARD

For Fancy cannot live on real food:
In youth she will despise familiar joy
To dwell in mournful shades; as they grow real,
Then buildeth she of joy her far ideal.

GODFREY

And so perverteth all. This stream to me
Sings, and in sunny ripples lingeringly
The water saith 'Ah me! where have I lept?
Into what garden of life? what banks are these,
What secret lawns, what ancient towers and trees?
Where the young sons of heav'n, with shouts of play
Or low delighted speech, welcome the day,
As if the poetry of the earth had slept
To wake in ecstasy. O stay me! alas!
Stay me, ye happy isles, ere that I pass
Without a memory on my sullen course
By the black city to the tossing seas!'

RICHARD

So might this old oak say, 'My heart is sere;
With greater effort every year I force
My stubborn leafage: soon my branch will crack,
And I shall fall or perish in the wrack:
And here another tree its crown will rear,
And see for centuries the boys at play:
And 'neath its boughs, on some fine holiday,
Old men shall prate as these.' Come and see the
    game.

GODFREY

Yes, if you will. 'Tis all one picture fair.

RICHARD

Made in a mirror, and who looketh there
Must see himself. Is not a dream the same?

GODFREY

Life is a dream.

RICHARD

                And you, who say it, seem
Dreaming to speak to a phantom in a dream.

Flycatchers

Sweet pretty fledgelings, perched on the rail arow,
Expectantly happy, where ye can watch below
Your parents a-hunting i' the meadow grasses
All the gay morning to feed you with flies;

Ye recall me a time sixty summers ago,
When, a young chubby chap, I sat just so
With others on a school-form rank'd in a row,
Not less eager and hungry than you, I trow,
With intelligences agape and eyes aglow,
While an authoritative old wise-acre
Stood over us and from a desk fed us with flies.

   Dead flies – such as litter the library south-window,
That buzzed at the panes until they fell stiff-baked on the sill,
Or are roll'd up asleep i' the blinds at sunrise,
Or wafer'd flat in a shrunken folio.

   A dry biped he was, nurtured likewise
On skins and skeletons, stale from top to toe
With all manner of rubbish and all manner of lies.

The Tramps

A schoolboy lay one night a-bed
    Under his window wide,
When dusk is lovelier than day
    In the high summertide;

The jasmin neath the casement throng'd
    Its ivory stars abloom;
With freaking peas and mignonette
    Their perfume fill'd the room:

Across the garden and beyond
    He look'd out on the skies,
And through black elmen boughs afar
    Watch'd where the moon should rise:

A warm rain fed the thirsty earth,
    Drops patter'd from the eaves
And from the tall trees as the shower
    Fell lisping on their leaves:

His heart was full, and pleasant thoughts
    Made music in his mind,
Like separate songs of birds, that are
    By general joy combined.

It seem'd the hour had gather'd up
    For every sense a bliss
To crown the faith of all desire
    With one assuaging kiss;

So that he fought with sleep to hold
   The rapture while he might,
Lest it should sink and drowning die
   Into the blank of night;

Nor kenn'd it was no passing thing
   Nor ever should be pass'd
But with him bide a joy to be
   As long as Life should last.

For though young thoughts be quite forgone,
   The pleasure of their dream
Can mesh them in its living mood
   And draw them in the stream:

So I can fancy when I will
   That there I lie intent
To hear the gentle whispering rain
   And drink the jasmin scent:

And then there sounds a distant tread
   Of men, that night who strode
Along the highway step by step
   Approaching down the road,

A company of three or four
   That hastening home again
After a Sabbath holiday
   Came talking in the rain:

Aloof from all my world and me
  They pass aneath the wall,
Till voice and footstep die away
  And into silence fall:

Into the maze of my delight
  Those blind intruders walk;
And ever I wonder who they be
  And of what things they talk.

Indolence

We left the city when the summer day
Had verged already on its hot decline,
And charmèd Indolence in languor lay
In her gay gardens, 'neath her towers divine:
'Farewell,' we said, 'dear city of youth and dream!'
And in our boat we stepped and took the stream.

All through that idle afternoon we strayed
Upon our proposed travel well begun,
As loitering by the woodland's dreamy shade,
Past shallow islets floating in the sun,
Or searching down the banks for rarer flowers
We lingered out the pleasurable hours.

Till when that loveliest came, which mowers home
Turns from their longest labour, as we steered
Along a straitened channel flecked with foam,
We lost our landscape wide, and slowly neared
An ancient bridge, that like a blind wall lay
Low on its buried vaults to block the way.

Then soon the narrow tunnels broader showed,
Where with its arches three it sucked the mass
Of water, that in swirl thereunder flowed,
Or stood piled at the piers waiting to pass;
And pulling for the middle span, we drew
The tender blades aboard and floated through.

But past the bridge what change we found below!
The stream, that all day long had laughed and played
Betwixt the happy shires, ran dark and slow,
And with its easy flood no murmur made:
And weeds spread on its surface, and about
The stagnant margin reared their stout heads out.

Upon the left high elms, with giant wood
Skirting the water-meadows, interwove
Their slumbrous crowns, o'ershadowing where they stood
The floor and heavy pillars of the grove:
And in the shade, through reeds and sedges dank,
A footpath led along the moated bank.

Across, all down the right, an old brick wall,
Above and o'er the channel, red did lean;
Here buttressed up, and bulging there to fall,
Tufted with grass and plants and lichen green;
And crumbling to the flood, which at its base
Slid gently nor disturbed its mirrored face.

Sheer on the wall the houses rose, their backs
All windowless, neglected and awry,
With tottering coigns, and crooked chimney stacks;
And here and there an unused door, set high
Above the fragments of its mouldering stair,
With rail and broken step led out on air.

Beyond, deserted wharfs and vacant sheds,
With empty boats and barges moored along,
And rafts half-sunken, fringed with weedy shreds,
And sodden beams, once soaked to season strong.
No sight of man, nor sight of life, no stroke,
No voice the somnolence and silence broke.

Then I who rowed leant on my oar, whose drip
Fell without sparkle, and I rowed no more;
And he that steered moved neither hand nor lip,
But turned his wondering eye from shore to shore;
And our trim boat let her swift motion die,
Between the dim reflections floating by.

Elegy

The wood is bare: a river-mist is steeping
  The trees that winter's chill of life bereaves:
Only their stiffened boughs break silence, weeping
    Over their fallen leaves;

That lie upon the dank earth brown and rotten,
  Miry and matted in the soaking wet:
Forgotten with the spring, that is forgotten
    By them that can forget.

Yet it was here we walked when ferns were springing,
  And through the mossy bank shot bud and blade:–
Here found in summer, when the birds were singing,
    A green and pleasant shade.

'Twas here we loved in sunnier days and greener;
  And now, in this disconsolate decay,
I come to see her where I most have seen her,
    And touch the happier day.

For on this path, at every turn and corner,
  The fancy of her figure on me falls:
Yet walks she with the slow step of a mourner,
    Nor hears my voice that calls.

So through my heart there winds a track of feeling,
  A path of memory, that is all her own:
Whereto her phantom beauty ever stealing
    Haunts the sad spot alone.

About her steps the trunks are bare, the branches
   Drip heavy tears upon her downcast head;
And bleed from unseen wounds that no sun stanches,
    For the year's sun is dead.

And dead leaves wrap the fruits that summer planted:
   And birds that love the South have taken wing.
The wanderer, loitering o'er the scene enchanted,
    Weeps, and despairs of spring.

'Poor withered rose and dry'

Poor withered rose and dry,
    Skeleton of a rose,
Risen to testify
    To love's sad close:

Treasured for love's sweet sake,
    That of joy past
Thou might'st again awake
    Memory at last.

Yet is thy perfume sweet;
    Thy petals red
Yet tell of summer heat,
    And the gay bed:

Yet, yet recall the glow
    Of the gazing sun,
When at thy bush we two
    Joined hands in one.

But, rose, thou hast not seen,
    Thou hast not wept
The change that passed between,
    Whilst thou hast slept.

To me thou seemest yet
    The dead dream's thrall:
While I live and forget
    Dream, truth and all.

Thou art more fresh than I,
    Rose, sweet and red:
Salt on my pale cheeks lie
    The tears I shed.

'I never shall love the snow again'

I never shall love the snow again
      Since Maurice died:
With corniced drift it blocked the lane
And sheeted in a desolate plain
      The country side.

The trees with silvery rime bedight
      Their branches bare.
By day no sun appeared; by night
The hidden moon shed thievish light
      In the misty air.

We fed the birds that flew around
      In flocks to be fed:
No shelter in holly or brake they found.
The speckled thrush on the frozen ground
      Lay frozen and dead.

We skated on stream and pond; we cut
      The crinching snow
To Doric temple or Arctic hut;
We laughed and sang at nightfall, shut
      By the fireside glow.

Yet grudged we our keen delights before
      Maurice should come.
We said, In-door or out-of-door
We shall love life for a month or more,
      When he is home.

They brought him home; 'twas two days late
    For Christmas day:
Wrapped in white, in solemn state,
A flower in his hand, all still and straight
    Our Maurice lay.

And two days ere the year outgave
    We laid him low.
The best of us truly were not brave,
When we laid Maurice down in his grave
    Under the snow.

On a Dead Child

Perfect little body, without fault or stain on thee,
   With promise of strength and manhood full and fair!
      Though cold and stark and bare,
The bloom and the charm of life doth awhile remain on thee.

Thy mother's treasure wert thou; – alas! no longer
   To visit her heart with wondrous joy; to be
      Thy father's pride; – ah, he
Must gather his faith together, and his strength make stronger.

To me, as I move thee now in the last duty,
   Dost thou with a turn or gesture anon respond;
      Startling my fancy fond
With a chance attitude of the head, a freak of beauty.

Thy hand clasps, as 'twas wont, my finger, and holds it:
   But the grasp is the clasp of Death, heartbreaking and stiff;
      Yet feels to my hand as if
'Twas still thy will, thy pleasure and trust that enfolds it.

So I lay thee there, thy sunken eyelids closing, –
   Go lie thou there in thy coffin, thy last little bed! –
      Propping thy wise, sad head,
Thy firm, pale hands across thy chest disposing.

So quiet! doth the change content thee? – Death, whither
   hath he taken thee?
   To a world, do I think, that rights the disaster of this?
      The vision of which I miss,

Who weep for the body, and wish but to warm thee and
   awaken thee?

Ah! little at best can all our hopes avail us
   To lift this sorrow, or cheer us, when in the dark,
         Unwilling, alone we embark,
And the things we have seen and have known and have
   heard of, fail us.

'The north wind came up yesternight'

The north wind came up yesternight
   With the new year's full moon,
And rising as she gained her height,
   Grew to a tempest soon.
Yet found he not on heaven's face
   A task of cloud to clear;
There was no speck that he might chase
   Off the blue hemisphere,
Nor vapour from the land to drive:
   The frost-bound country held
Nought motionable or alive,
   That 'gainst his wrath rebelled.
There scarce was hanging in the wood
   A shrivelled leaf to reave;
No bud had burst its swathing hood
   That he could rend or grieve:
Only the tall tree-skeletons,
   Where they were shadowed all,
Wavered a little on the stones,
   And on the white church-wall.

– Like as an artist in his mood,
    Who reckons all as nought,
So he may quickly paint his nude,
    Unutterable thought:
So Nature in a frenzied hour
    By day or night will show
Dim indications of the power
    That doometh man to woe.
Ah, many have my visions been,
    And some I know full well:
I would that all that I have seen
    Were fit for speech to tell. –

And by the churchyard as I came,
    It seemed my spirit passed
Into a land that hath no name,
    Grey, melancholy and vast;
Where nothing comes: but Memory,
    The widowed queen of Death,
Reigns, and with fixed, sepulchral eye
    All slumber banisheth.
Each grain of writhen dust, that drapes
    That sickly, staring shore,
Its old chaotic change of shapes
    Remembers evermore.
And ghosts of cities long decayed,
    And ruined shrines of Fate
Gather the paths, that Time hath made
    Foolish and desolate.
Nor winter there hath hope of spring,
    Nor the pale night of day,
Since the old king with scorpion sting
    Hath done himself away.

*   *   *

The morn was calm; the wind's last breath
    Had fal'n: in solemn hush
The golden moon went down beneath
    The dawning's crimson flush.

Recollections of Solitude

AN ELEGY

Ended are many days, and now but few
Remain; since therefore it is happy and true
That memoried joys keep ever their delight,
Like steadfast stars in the blue vault of night,
While hours of pain (among those heavenly spheres
Like falling meteors, the martyr's tears)
Dart their long trails at random, and anon,
Ere we exclaim, pass, and for aye are gone;
Therefore my heedy thought will oft restore
The long light-hearted days that are no more,
Save where in her memorial crypt they shine
Spangling the silent past with joy divine.

But why in dream of this enchanted mood
Should all my boyhood seem a solitude?
Good reason know I, when I wander there,
In that transmuted scene, why all is fair;
The woods as when in holiday of spring
Million buds burst, and flowers are blossoming;
The meadows deep in grass, the fields unshorn
In beauty of the multitudinous corn,
Where the strait alleys hide me, wall'd between
High bloomy stalks and rustling banners green;
The gardens, too, in dazzling hues full-blown,
With wafted scent and blazing petals strewn;
The orchards reddening thro' the patient hours,
While idle autumn in his mossy bowers
Inviteth meditation to endear
The sanctuaries of the mellowing year;

And every spot wherein I loved to stray
Hath borrowed radiance of eternal day;
But why am I ever alone, alone?
Here in the corner of a field my throne,
Now in the branching chair of some tall tree
Drinking the gale in bird-like liberty;
Or to the seashore wandered in the sun
To watch the fateful waves break one by one;
Or if on basking downs supine I lie
Bathing my spirit in blue calms of the sky;
Or to the river bank am stolen by night
Hearkening unto the moonlit ripple bright
That warbles o'er the shallows of smooth stone;
Why should my memory find me all alone,
When I had such companions every day
Jocund and dear? 'Twixt glimpses of their play
'Tis a vast solitude, wherein I see
Only myself and what I came to be.

Yet never think, dear spirits, if now ye may
Remember aught of that brief earthly day,
Ere ye the mournful Stygian river crost,
From our familiar home too early lost, –
O never think that I your tears forget,
Or that I loved not well, or love not yet.
Nor ye who held my heart in passion's chain, –
As kings and queens succeed in glorious reign –
When, as a man, I made you to outvie
God's work, and, as a god, then set you by
Among the sainted throng in holiest shrine
Of mythic creed and poetry divine;
True was my faith, and still your loves endure,
The jewels of my fancy, bright and pure.

Nor only in fair places do I see
The picture fair now it has ceased to be:
For fate once led me, and myself some days
Did I devote, to dull laborious ways,
By soaring thought detained to tread full low, –
Yea might I say unbeauteous paths of woe
And dreary abodes, had not my youthful sprite
Hallow'd each nook with legends of delight.

Ah! o'er that smoky town who looketh now
By winter sunset from the dark hill-brow,
Under the dying trees exultantly
Nursing the sting of human tragedy?
Or in that little room upstair'd so high,
Where London's roofs in thickest huddle lie,
Who now returns at evening to entice
To his fireside the joys of Paradise?
Once sacred was that hearth, and bright the air;
The flame of man's redemption flickered there,
In worship of those spirits, whose deathless fames
Have thrilled the stars of heaven to hear their names;
They that excell'd in wisdom to create
Beauty, with mortal passion conquering fate;
And, mid the sovran powers of elder time,
The loveliness of music and new rhyme,
The masters young that first enthrallèd me;
Of whom if I should name, whom then but thee,
Sweet Shelley, or the boy whose book was found
Thrust in thy bosom on thy body drowned?

Oh mighty Muse, wooer of virgin thought,
Beside thy charm all else counteth as nought;
The revelation of thy smile doth make
Him whom thou lovest reckless for thy sake;

Earthborn of suffering, that knowest well
To call thine own, and with enamouring spell
Feedest the stolen powers of godlike youth
On dear imagination's only truth,
Building with song a temple of desire;
And with the yearning music of thy quire,
In nuptial sacrament of thought and sense
Hallowest for toil the hours of indolence:
Thou in thy melancholic beauty drest,
Subduest ill to serve thy fair behest,
With tragic tears, and sevenfold purified
Silver of mirth; and with extremest pride,
With secret doctrine and unfathomed lore
Remainest yet a child for evermore,
The only enchantress of the earth that art
To cheer his day and staunch man's bleeding heart.

O heavenly Muse, for heavenly thee we call
Who in the fire of love refinest all,
Accurst is he who heark'neth not thy voice;
But happy he who, numbered of thy choice,
Walketh aloof from nature's clouded plan:
For all God's world is but the thought of man;
Wherein has thou re-formed a world apart,
The mutual mirror of his better heart.
There is no foulness, misery, nor sin,
But he who loves finds his desire therein,
And there with thee in lonely commerce lives:
Nay, all that nature gave or fortune gives,
Joys that his spirit is most jealous of,
His only-embraced and best-deserving love,
Who walketh in the noon of heavenly praise,
The troubled godhead of his children's gaze,

Wear thine eternity, and are loved best
By thee transfigured and in thee possest;
Who madest beauty, and from thy boundless store
Of beauty shalt create for evermore.

1900

The Sleeping Mansion

As our car rustled swiftly
    along the village lane,
we caught sight for a moment
    of the old house again,

Which once I made my home in –
    ev'n as a soul may dwell
enamouring the body
    that she loveth so well:

But I long since had left it;
    what fortune now befals
finds me on other meadows
    by other trees and walls.

The place look'd blank and empty,
    a sleeper's witless face
which to his mind's enchantment
    is numb, and gives no trace.

And to that slumbering mansion
    was I come as a dream,
to cheer her in her stupor
    and loneliness extreme.

I knew what sudden wonder
    I brought her in my flight;
what rapturous joy possess'd her,
    what peace and soft delight.

Cheddar Pinks

Mid the squander'd colour
   idling as I lay
Reading the Odyssey
   in my rock-garden
I espied the cluster'd
   tufts of Cheddar pinks
Burgeoning with promise
   of their scented bloom
All the modish motley
   of their bloom to-be
Thrust up in narrow buds
   on the slender stalks
Thronging springing urgent
   hasting (so I thought)
As if they fear'd to be
   too late for summer –
Like schoolgirls overslept
   waken'd by the bell
Leaping from bed to don
   their muslin dresses
     On a May morning:

Then felt I like to one
   indulging in sin
(Whereto Nature is oft
   a blind accomplice)
Because my aged bones
   so enjoy'd the sun
There as I lay alone
   idling with my thoughts

[50]

Reading an old poet
   while the busy world
Toil'd moil'd fuss'd and scurried
   worried bought and sold
Plotted stole and quarrel'd
   fought and God knows what.
I had forgotten Homer
   dallying with my thoughts
Till I fell to making
   these little verses
Communing with the flowers
   in my rock-garden
     On a May morning.

Reflections on Life
and Art

'I love all beauteous things'

I love all beauteous things,
   I seek and adore them;
God hath no better praise,
And man in his hasty days
   Is honoured for them.

I too will something make
   And joy in the making;
Altho' to-morrow it seem
Like the empty words of a dream
   Remembered on waking.

'O my vague desires!'

O my vague desires!
Ye lambent flames of the soul, her offspring fires:
That are my soul herself in pangs sublime
Rising and flying to heaven before her time:

What doth tempt you forth
To drown in the south or shiver in the frosty north?
What seek ye or find ye in your random flying,
Ever soaring aloft, soaring and dying?

Joy, the joy of flight!
They hide in the sun, they flare and dance in the night;
Gone up, gone out of sight: and ever again
Follow fresh tongues of fire, fresh pangs of pain.

Ah! they burn my soul,
The fires, devour my soul that once was whole:
She is scattered in fiery phantoms day by day,
But whither, whither? ay whither? away, away!

Could I but control
These vague desires, these leaping flames of the soul:
Could I but quench the fire: ah! could I stay
My soul that flieth, alas, and dieth away!

'I have loved flowers that fade'

I have loved flowers that fade,
Within whose magic tents
Rich hues have marriage made
With sweet unmemoried scents:
A honeymoon delight, –
A joy of love at sight,
That ages in an hour: –
My song be like a flower!

I have loved airs, that die
Before their charm is writ
Along a liquid sky
Trembling to welcome it.
Notes, that with pulse of fire
Proclaim the spirit's desire,
Then die, and are nowhere: –
My song be like an air!

Die, song, die like a breath,
And wither as a bloom:
Fear not a flowery death,
Dread not an airy tomb!
Fly with delight, fly hence!
'Twas thine love's tender sense
To feast; now on thy bier
Beauty shall shed a tear.

'Haste on, my joys!'

Haste on, my joys! your treasure lies
   In swift, unceasing flight.
O haste: for while your beauty flies
   I seize your full delight.
Lo! I have seen the scented flower,
   Whose tender stems I cull,
For her brief date and meted hour
   Appear more beautiful.

O youth, O strength, O most divine
   For that so short ye prove;
Were but your rare gifts longer mine,
   Ye scarce would win my love.
Nay, life itself the heart would spurn,
   Did once the days restore
The days, that once enjoyed return,
   Return – ah! nevermore.

Spring

ODE I

Invitation to the Country

Again with pleasant green
Has Spring renewed the wood,
And where the bare trunks stood
Are leafy arbours seen;
And back on budding boughs
Come birds, to court and pair,
Whose rival amorous vows
Amaze the scented air.

The freshets are unbound,
And leaping from the hill,
Their mossy banks refill
With streams of light and sound:
And scattered down the meads,
From hour to hour unfold
A thousand buds and beads
In stars and cups of gold.

Now hear, and see, and note,
The farms are all astir,
And every labourer
Has doffed his winter coat;
And how with specks of white
They dot the brown hillside,
Or jaunt and sing outright
As by their teams they stride.

They sing to feel the Sun
Regain his wanton strength;
To know the year at length
Rewards their labour done;
To see the rootless stake
They set bare in the ground,
Burst into leaf, and shake
Its grateful scent around.

Ah now an evil lot
Is his, who toils for gain,
Where crowded chimneys stain
The heavens his choice forgot;
'Tis on the blighted trees
That deck his garden dim,
And in the tainted breeze,
That sweet Spring comes to him.

Far sooner I would choose
The life of brutes that bask,
Than set myself a task,
Which inborn powers refuse:
And rather far enjoy
The body, than invent
A duty, to destroy
The ease which nature sent;

And country life I praise,
And lead, because I find
The philosophic mind
Can take no middle ways;
She will not leave her love
To mix with men, her art
Is all to strive above
The crowd, or stand apart.

Thrice happy he, the rare
Prometheus, who can play
With hidden things, and lay
New realms of nature bare;
Whose venturous step has trod
Hell underfoot, and won
A crown from man and God
For all that he has done. –

That highest gift of all,
Since crabbèd fate did flood
My heart with sluggish blood,
I look not mine to call;
But, like a truant freed,
Fly to the woods, and claim
A pleasure for the deed
Of my inglorious name:

And am content, denied
The best, in choosing right;
For Nature can delight
Fancies unoccupied
With ecstasies so sweet
As none can even guess,
Who walk not with the feet
Of joy in idleness.

Then leave your joyless ways,
My friend, my joys to see.
The day you come shall be
The choice of chosen days:
You shall be lost, and learn
New being, and forget
The world, till your return
Shall bring your first regret.

Spring

ODE II

Reply

Behold! the radiant Spring,
In splendour decked anew,
Down from her heaven of blue
Returns on sunlit wing:
The zephyrs of her train
In fleecy clouds disport,
And birds to greet her reign
Summon their silvan court.

And here in street and square
The prisoned trees contest
Her favour with the best,
To robe themselves full fair:
And forth their buds provoke,
Forgetting winter brown,
And all the mire and smoke
That wrapped the dingy town.

Now he that loves indeed
His pleasure must awake,
Lest any pleasure take
Its flight, and he not heed;
For of his few short years
Another now invites
His hungry soul, and cheers
His life with new delights.

And who loves Nature more
Than he, whose painful art
Has taught and skilled his heart
To read her skill and lore?
Whose spirit leaps more high,
Plucking the pale primrose,
Than his whose feet must fly
The pasture where it grows?

One long in city pent
Forgets, or must complain:
But think not I can stain
My heaven with discontent;
Nor wallow with that sad,
Backsliding herd, who cry
That Truth must make man bad,
And pleasure is a lie.

Rather while Reason lives
To mark me from the beast,
I'll teach her serve at least
To heal the wound she gives:
Nor need she strain her powers
Beyond a common flight,
To make the passing hours
Happy from morn till night.

Since health our toil rewards,
And strength is labour's prize,
I hate not, nor despise
The work my lot accords;
Nor fret with fears unkind
The tender joys, that bless
My hard-won peace of mind,
In hours of idleness.

Then what charm company
Can give, know I, – if wine
Go round, or throats combine
To set dumb music free.
Or deep in wintertide
When winds without make moan,
I love my own fireside
Not least when most alone.

Then oft I turn the page
In which our country's name,
Spoiling the Greek of fame,
Shall sound in every age:
Or some Terentian play
Renew, whose excellent
Adjusted folds betray
How once Menander went.

    Or if grave study suit
The yet unwearied brain,
Plato can teach again,
And Socrates dispute;
Till fancy in a dream
Confront their souls with mine,
Crowning the mind supreme,
And her delights divine.

    While pleasure yet can be
Pleasant, and fancy sweet,
I bid all care retreat
From my philosophy;
Which, when I come to try
Your simpler life, will find,
I doubt not, joys to vie
With those I leave bchind.

The Voice of Nature

I stand on the cliff and watch the veiled sun paling
    A silver field afar in the mournful sea,
The scourge of the surf, and plaintive gulls sailing
    At ease on the gale that smites the shuddering lea:
             Whose smile severe and chaste
    June never hath stirred to vanity, nor age defaced.
In lofty thought strive, O spirit, for ever:
In courage and strength pursue thine own endeavour.

Ah! if it were only for thee, thou restless ocean
    Of waves that follow and roar, the sweep of the tides;
Wer't only for thee, impetuous wind, whose motion
    Precipitate all o'errides, and turns, nor abides:
             For you sad birds and fair,
    Or only for thee, bleak cliff, erect in the air;
Then well could I read wisdom in every feature,
O well should I understand the voice of Nature.

But far away, I think, in the Thames valley,
    The silent river glides by flowery banks:
And birds sing sweetly in branches that arch an alley
    Of cloistered trees, moss-grown in their ancient ranks:
             Where if a light air stray,
    'Tis laden with hum of bees and scent of may.
Love and peace be thine, O spirit, for ever:
Serve thy sweet desire: despise endeavour.

And if it were only for thee, entrancèd river,
    That scarce dost rock the lily on her airy stem,
Or stir a wave to murmur, or a rush to quiver;
    Wer't but for the woods, and summer asleep in them:
            For you my bowers green,
    My hedges of rose and woodbine, with walks between,
Then well could I read wisdom in every feature,
O well should I understand the voice of Nature.

'Riding adown the country lanes'

Riding adown the country lanes
    One day in spring,
Heavy at heart with all the pains
  Of man's imagining: –

The mist was not yet melted quite
    Into the sky:
The small round sun was dazzling white,
  The merry larks sang high:

The grassy northern slopes were laid
    In sparkling dew,
Out of the slow-retreating shade
  Turning from sleep anew:

Deep in the sunny vale a burn
    Ran with the lane,
O'erhung with ivy, moss and fern
  It laughed in joyful strain:

And primroses shot long and lush
    Their cluster'd cream:
Robin and wren and amorous thrush
  Carol'd above the stream:

The stillness of the lenten air
    Call'd into sound
The motions of all life that were
  In field and farm around:

So fair it was, so sweet and bright,
    The jocund Spring
Awoke in me the old delight
  Of man's imagining,

Riding adown the country lanes:
    The larks sang high. –
O heart! for all thy griefs and pains
  Thou shalt be loth to die.

'I would be a bird'

I would be a bird, and straight on wings I arise,
And carry purpose up to the ends of the air:
In calm and storm my sails I feather, and where
By freezing cliffs the unransom'd wreckage lies:
Or, strutting on hot meridian banks, surprise
The silence: over plains in the moonlight bare
I chase my shadow, and perch where no bird dare
In treetops torn by fiercest winds of the skies.

    Poor simple birds, foolish birds! then I cry,
Ye pretty pictures of delight, unstir'd
By the only joy of knowing that ye fly;
Ye are not what ye are, but rather, sum'd in a word,
The alphabet of a god's idea, and I
Who master it, I am the only bird.

'The sea keeps not the Sabbath day'

The sea keeps not the Sabbath day,
His waves come rolling evermore;
His noisy toil grindeth the shore,
And all the cliff is drencht with spray.

Here as we sit, my love and I,
Under the pine upon the hill,
The sadness of the clouded sky,
The bitter wind, the gloomy roar,
The seamew's melancholy cry
With loving fancy suit but ill.

We talk of moons and cooling suns,
Of geologic time and tide,
The eternal sluggards that abide
While our fair love so swiftly runs,

Of nature that doth half consent
That man should guess her dreary scheme
Lest he should live too well content
In his fair house of mirth and dream:

Whose labour irks his ageing heart,
His heart that wearies of desire,
Being so fugitive a part
Of what so slowly must expire.

She in her agelong toil and care
Persistent, wearies not nor stays,
Mocking alike hope and despair.

– Ah, but she too can mock our praise,
Enchanted on her brighter days,

Days, that the thought of grief refuse,
Days that are one with human art,
Worthy of the Virgilian muse,
Fit for the gaiety of Mozart.

Elegy

AMONG THE TOMBS

Sad, sombre place, beneath whose antique yews
I come, unquiet sorrows to control;
Amid thy silent mossgrown graves to muse
With my neglected solitary soul;
And to poetic sadness care confide,
Trusting sweet Melancholy for my guide:

They will not ask why in thy shades I stray,
Among the tombs finding my rare delight,
Beneath the sun at indolent noonday,
Or in the windy moon-enchanted night,
Who have once reined in their steeds at any shrine,
And given them water from the well divine. –

   The orchards are all ripened, and the sun
Spots the deserted gleanings with decay;
The seeds are perfected: his work is done,
And Autumn lingers but to outsmile the May;
Bidding his tinted leaves glide, bidding clear
Unto clear skies the birds applaud the year.

Lo, here I sit, and to the world I call,
The world my solemn fancy leaves behind,
Come! pass within the inviolable wall,
Come pride, come pleasure, come distracted mind;
Within the fated refuge, hither, turn,
And learn your wisdom ere 'tis late to learn.

Come with me now, and taste the fount of tears;
For many eyes have sanctified this spot,
Where grief's unbroken lineage endears
The charm untimely Folly injures not,
And slays the intruding thoughts, that overleap
The simple fence its holiness doth keep.

Read the worn names of the forgotten dead,
Their pompous legends will no smile awake;
Even the vainglorious title o'er the head
Wins its pride pardon for its sorrow's sake;
And carven Loves scorn not their dusty prize,
Though fallen so far from tender sympathies.

Here where a mother laid her only son,
Here where a lover left his bride, below
The treasured names their own are added on
To those whom they have followed long ago:
Sealing the record of the tears they shed,
That 'where their treasure there their hearts are fled.'

Grandfather, father, son, and then again
Child, grandchild, and great-grandchild laid beneath
Numbered in turn among the sons of men,
And gathered each one in his turn to death:
While he that occupies their house and name
To-day, – to-morrow too their grave shall claim.

And where are all their spirits? Ah! could we tell
The manner of our being when we die,
And see beyond the scene we know so well
The country that so much obscured doth lie!
With brightest visions our fond hopes repair,
Or crown our melancholy with despair;

From death, still death, still would a comfort come:
Since of this world the essential joy must fall
In all distributed, in each thing some,
In nothing all, and all complete in all;
Till pleasure, ageing to her full increase,
Puts on perfection, and is throned in peace.

Yea, sweetest peace, unsought-for, undesired,
Loathed and misnamed, 'tis thee I worship here:
Though in most black habiliments attired,
Thou art sweet peace, and thee I cannot fear.
Nay, were my last hope quenched, I here would sit
And praise the annihilation of the pit.

Nor quickly disenchanted will my feet
Back to the busy town return, but yet
Linger, ere I my loving friends would greet,
Or touch their hands, or share without regret
The warmth of that kind hearth, whose sacred ties
Only shall dim with tears my dying eyes.

'Joy, sweetest lifeborn joy,
where dost thou dwell?'

Joy, sweetest lifeborn joy, where dost thou dwell?
Upon the formless moments of our being
Flitting, to mock the ear that heareth well,
To escape the trainèd eye that strains in seeing,
Dost thou fly with us whither we are fleeing;
Or home in our creations, to withstand
Black-wingèd death, that slays the making hand?

The making mind, that must untimely perish
Amidst its work which time may not destroy,
The beauteous forms which man shall love to cherish,
The glorious songs that combat earth's annoy?
Thou dost dwell here, I know, divinest Joy:
But they who build thy towers fair and strong,
Of all that toil, feel most of care and wrong.

Sense is so tender, O and hope so high,
That common pleasures mock their hope and sense;
And swifter than doth lightning from the sky
The ecstasy they pine for flashes hence,
Leaving the darkness and the woe immense,
Wherewith it seems no thread of life was woven,
Nor doth the track remain where once 'twas cloven.

And heaven and all the stable elements
That guard God's purpose mock us, though the mind
Be spent in searching: for his old intents
We see were never for our joy designed:
They shine as doth the bright sun on the blind,
Or like his pensioned stars, that hymn above
His praise, but not toward us, that God is Love.

[77]

For who so well hath wooed the maiden hours
As quite to have won the worth of their rich show,
To rob the night of mystery, or the flowers
Of their sweet delicacy ere they go?
Nay, even the dear occasion when we know,
We miss the joy, and on the gliding day
The special glories float and pass away.

Only life's common plod: still to repair
The body and the thing which perisheth:
The soil, the smutch, the toil and ache and wear,
The grinding enginry of blood and breath,
Pain's random darts, the heartless spade of death;
All is but grief, and heavily we call
On the last terror for the end of all.

Then comes the happy moment: not a stir
In any tree, no portent in the sky:
The morn doth neither hasten nor defer,
The morrow hath no name to call it by,
But life and joy are one, – we know not why, –
As though our very blood long breathless lain
Had tasted of the breath of God again.

And having tasted it I speak of it,
And praise him thinking how I trembled then
When his touch strengthened me, as now I sit
In wonder, reaching out beyond my ken,
Reaching to turn the day back, and my pen
Urging to tell a tale which told would seem
The witless phantasy of them that dream.

But O most blessèd truth, for truth thou art,
Abide thou with me till my life shall end.
Divinity hath surely touched my heart;
I have possessed more joy than earth can lend:
I may attain what time shall never spend.
Only let not my duller days destroy
The memory of thy witness and my joy.

The Affliction of Richard

Love not too much. But how,
When thou hast made me such,
And dost thy gifts bestow,
How can I love too much?
  Though I must fear to lose,
And drown my joy in care,
With all its thorns I choose
The path of love and prayer.

Though thou, I know not why,
Didst kill my childish trust,
That breach with toil did I
Repair, because I must:
  And spite of frighting schemes,
With which the fiends of Hell
Blaspheme thee in my dreams,
So far I have hoped well.

But what the heavenly key,
What marvel in me wrought
Shall quite exculpate thee,
I have no shadow of thought.
  What am I that complain?
The love, from which began
My question sad and vain,
Justifies thee to man.

'Weep not to-day:
why should this sadness be?'

Weep not to-day: why should this sadness be?
      Learn in present fears
      To o'ermaster those tears
      That unhindered conquer thee.

Think on thy past valour, thy future praise:
      Up, sad heart, nor faint
      In ungracious complaint,
      Or a prayer for better days.

Daily thy life shortens, the grave's dark peace
      Draweth surely nigh,
      When good-night is good-bye;
      For the sleeping shall not cease.

Fight, to be found fighting: nor far away
      Deem, nor strange thy doom.
      Like this sorrow 'twill come,
      And the day will be to-day.

The English Scene

January

Cold is the winter day, misty and dark:
  The sunless sky with faded gleams is rent;
And patches of thin snow outlying, mark
  The landscape with a drear disfigurement.

The trees their mournful branches lift aloft:
  The oak with knotty twigs is full of trust,
With bud-thronged bough the cherry in the croft;
  The chestnut holds her gluey knops upthrust.

No birds sing, but the starling chaps his bill
  And chatters mockingly; the newborn lambs
Within their strawbuilt fold beneath the hill
  Answer with plaintive cry their bleating dams.

Their voices melt in welcome dreams of spring,
  Green grass and leafy trees and sunny skies:
My fancy decks the woods, the thrushes sing,
  Meadows are gay, bees hum and scents arise.

And God the Maker doth my heart grow bold
  To praise for wintry works not understood,
Who all the worlds and ages doth behold,
  Evil and good as one, and all as good.

Last week of February, 1890

Hark to the merry birds, hark how they sing!
   Although 'tis not yet spring
     And keen the air;
Hale Winter, half resigning ere he go,
   Doth to his heiress shew
     His kingdom fair.

In patient russet is his forest spread,
   All bright with bramble red,
     With beechen moss
And holly sheen: the oak silver and stark
   Sunneth his aged bark
     And wrinkled boss.

But neath the ruin of the withered brake
   Primroses now awake
     From nursing shades:
The crumpled carpet of the dry leaves brown
   Avails not to keep down
     The hyacinth blades.

The hazel hath put forth his tassels ruffed;
   The willow's flossy tuft
     Hath slipped him free:
The rose amid her ransacked orange hips
   Braggeth the tender tips
     Of bowers to be.

A black rook stirs the branches here and there,
  Foraging to repair
    His broken home:
And hark, on the ash-boughs! Never thrush did sing
  Louder in praise of spring,
    When spring is come.

A Robin

Flame-throated robin on the topmost bough
  Of the leafless oak, what singest thou?
    Hark! he telleth how –
  'Spring is coming now; Spring is coming now.

Now ruddy are the elm-tops against the blue sky,
  The pale larch donneth her jewelry;
    Red fir and black fir sigh,
  And I am lamenting the year gone by.

The bushes where I nested are all cut down,
  They are felling the tall trees one by one,
    And my mate is dead and gone,
  In the winter she died and left me lone.

She lay in the thicket where I fear to go;
  For when the March-winds after the snow
    The leaves away did blow,
  She was not there, and my heart is woe:

And sad is my song, when I begin to sing,
  As I sit in the sunshine this merry spring:
    Like a withered leaf I cling
  To the white oak-bough, while the wood doth ring.

Spring is coming now, the sun again is gay;
  Each day like a last spring's happy day.' –
    Thus sang he; then from his spray
  He saw me listening and flew away.

The Palm Willow

See, whirling snow sprinkles the starvèd fields,
    The birds have stayed to sing;
No covert yet their fairy harbour yields.
      When cometh Spring?
Ah! in their tiny throats what songs unborn
     Are quenched each morn.

The lenten lilies, through the frost that push,
    Their yellow heads withhold:
The woodland willow stands a lonely bush
     Of nebulous gold;
There the Spring-goddess cowers in faint attire
     Of frightened fire.

April, 1885

Wanton with long delay the gay spring leaping cometh;
The blackthorn starreth now his bough on the eve of May:
All day in the sweet box-tree the bee for pleasure hummeth:
The cuckoo sends afloat his note on the air all day.

Now dewy nights again and rain in gentle shower
At root of tree and flower have quenched the winter's drouth:
On high the hot sun smiles, and banks of cloud uptower
In bulging heads that crowd for miles the dazzling south.

'I heard a linnet courting'

I heard a linnet courting
  His lady in the spring:
His mates were idly sporting,
  Nor stayed to hear him sing
    His song of love, –
I fear my speech distorting
    His tender love.

The phrases of his pleading
  Were full of young delight;
And she that gave him heeding
  Interpreted aright
    His gay, sweet notes, –
So sadly marred in the reading, –
    His tender notes.

And when he ceased, the hearer
  Awaited the refrain,
Till swiftly perching nearer
  He sang his song again,
    His pretty song: –
Would that my verse spake clearer
    His tender song!

Ye happy, airy creatures!
  That in the merry spring
Think not of what misfeatures
  Or cares the year may bring;
    But unto love
Resign your simple natures,
    To tender love.

[91]

'Spring goeth all in white'

Spring goeth all in white,
Crowned with milk-white may:
In fleecy flocks of light
O'er heaven the white clouds stray:

   White butterflies in the air;
White daisies prank the ground:
The cherry and hoary pear
Scatter their snow around.

'The hill pines were sighing'

The hill pines were sighing,
O'ercast and chill was the day:
A mist in the valley lying
Blotted the pleasant May.

But deep in the glen's bosom
Summer slept in the fire
Of the odorous gorse-blossom
And the hot scent of the brier.

A ribald cuckoo clamoured,
And out of the copse the stroke
Of the iron axe that hammered
The iron heart of the oak.

Anon a sound appalling,
As a hundred years of pride
Crashed, in the silence falling:
And the shadowy pine-trees sighed.

Nightingales

Beautiful must be the mountains whence ye come,
  And bright in the fruitful valleys the streams, wherefrom
      Ye learn your song:
Where are those starry woods? O might I wander there,
  Among the flowers, which in that heavenly air
      Bloom the year long!

Nay, barren are those mountains and spent the streams:
  Our song is the voice of desire, that haunts our dreams,
      A throe of the heart,
Whose pining visions dim, forbidden hopes profound,
  No dying cadence nor long sigh can sound,
      For all our art.

Alone, aloud in the raptured ear of men
  We pour our dark nocturnal secret; and then,
      As night is withdrawn
From these sweet-springing meads and bursting boughs of
  May,
  Dream, while the innumerable choir of day
      Welcome the dawn.

'The summer trees are tempest-torn'

The summer trees are tempest-torn,
The hills are wrapped in a mantle wide
Of folding rain by the mad wind borne
    Across the country side.

His scourge of fury is lashing down
The delicate-rankèd golden corn,
That never more shall rear its crown
    And curtsey to the morn.

There shews no care in heaven to save
Man's pitiful patience, or provide
A season for the season's slave,
    Whose trust hath toiled and died.

So my proud spirit in me is sad,
A wreck of fairer fields to mourn,
The ruin of golden hopes she had,
    My delicate-rankèd corn.

'The pinks along my garden walks'

The pinks along my garden walks
Have all shot forth their summer stalks,
Thronging their buds 'mong tulips hot,
    And blue forget-me-not.

Their dazzling snows forth-bursting soon
Will lade the idle breath of June:
And waken thro' the fragrant night
    To steal the pale moonlight.

The nightingale at end of May
Lingers each year for their display;
Till when he sees their blossoms blown,
    He knows the spring is flown.

June's birth they greet, and when their bloom
Dislustres, withering on his tomb,
Then summer hath a shortening day;
    And steps slow to decay.

'The storm is over,
the land hushes to rest'

The storm is over, the land hushes to rest:
The tyrannous wind, its strength fordone,
Is fallen back in the west
To couch with the sinking sun.
The last clouds fare
With fainting speed, and their thin streamers fly
In melting drifts of the sky.
Already the birds in the air
Appear again; the rooks return to their haunt,
And one by one,
Proclaiming aloud their care,
Renew their peaceful chant.

Torn and shattered the trees their branches again reset,
They trim afresh the fair
Few green and golden leaves withheld from the storm,
And awhile will be handsome yet.
To-morrow's sun shall caress
Their remnant of loveliness:
In quiet days for a time
Sad Autumn lingering warm
Shall humour their faded prime.

But ah! the leaves of summer that lie on the ground!
What havoc! The laughing timbrels of June,
That curtained the birds' cradles, and screened their song,
That sheltered the cooing doves at noon,
Of airy fans the delicate throng, –
Torn and scattered around:

Far out afield they lie,
In the watery furrows die,
In grassy pools of the flood they sink and drown,
Green-golden, orange, vermilion, golden and brown,
The high year's flaunting crown
Shattered and trampled down.

The day is done: the tired land looks for night:
She prays to the night to keep
In peace her nerves of delight:
While silver mist upstealeth silently,
And the broad cloud-driving moon in the clear sky
Lifts o'er the firs her shining shield,
And in her tranquil light
Sleep falls on forest and field.
Sée! sléep hath fallen: the trees are asleep:
The night is come. The land is wrapt in sleep.

The Downs

O bold majestic downs, smooth, fair and lonely;
O still solitude, only matched in the skies:
    Perilous in steep places,
    Soft in the level races,
Where sweeping in phantom silence the cloudland flies;
With lovely undulation of fall and rise;
    Entrenched with thickets thorned,
By delicate miniature dainty flowers adorned!

I climb your crown, and lo! a sight surprising
Of sea in front uprising, steep and wide:
    And scattered ships ascending
    To heaven, lost in the blending
Of distant blues, where water and sky divide,
Urging their engines against wind and tide,
    And all so small and slow
They seem to be wearily pointing the way they would go.

The accumulated murmur of soft plashing,
Of waves on rocks dashing and searching the sands,
    Takes my ear, in the veering
    Baffled wind, as rearing
Upright at the cliff, to the gullies and rifts he stands;
And his conquering surges scour out over the lands;
    While again at the foot of the downs
He masses his strength to recover the topmost crowns.

'The upper skies are palest blue'

The upper skies are palest blue
Mottled with pearl and fretted snow:
With tattered fleece of inky hue
Close overhead the storm-clouds go.

Their shadows fly along the hill
And o'er the crest mount one by one:
The whitened planking of the mill
Is now in shade and now in sun.

'The clouds have left the sky'

The clouds have left the sky,
The wind hath left the sea,
The half-moon up on high
Shrinketh her face of dree.

She lightens on the comb
Of leaden waves, that roar
And thrust their hurried foam
Up on the dusky shore.

Behind the western bars
The shrouded day retreats,
And unperceived the stars
Steal to their sovran seats.

And whiter grows the foam,
The small moon lightens more;
And as I turn me home,
My shadow walks before.

'A poppy grows upon the shore'

A poppy grows upon the shore,
Bursts her twin cup in summer late:
Her leaves are glaucous-green and hoar,
Her petals yellow, delicate.

Oft to her cousins turns her thought,
In wonder if they care that she
Is fed with spray for dew, and caught
By every gale that sweeps the sea.

She has no lovers like the red,
That dances with the noble corn:
Her blossoms on the waves are shed,
Where she stands shivering and forlorn.

The Windmill

The green corn waving in the dale,
The ripe grass waving on the hill:
I lean across the paddock pale
And gaze upon the giddy mill.

Its hurtling sails a mighty sweep
Cut thro' the air: with rushing sound
Each strikes in fury down the steep,
Rattles, and whirls in chase around.

Beside his sacks the miller stands
On high within the open door:
A book and pencil in his hands,
His grist and meal he reckoneth o'er.

His tireless merry slave the wind
Is busy with his work to-day:
From whencesoe'er, he comes to grind;
He hath a will and knows the way.

He gives the creaking sails a spin,
The circling millstones faster flee,
The shuddering timbers groan within,
And down the shoot the meal runs free.

The miller giveth him no thanks,
And doth not much his work o'erlook:
He stands beside the sacks, and ranks
The figures in his dusty book.

Larks

What voice of gladness, hark!
   In heaven is ringing?
From the sad fields the lark
   Is upward winging.

High through the mournful mist that blots our day
Their songs betray them soaring in the grey.
   See them! Nay, they
In sunlight swim; above the furthest stain
Of cloud attain; their hearts in music rain
   Upon the plain.

Sweet birds, far out of sight
   Your songs of pleasure
Dome us with joy as bright
   As heaven's best azure.

The Winnowers

Betwixt two billows of the downs
   The little hamlet lies,
And nothing sees but the bald crowns
   Of the hills, and the blue skies.

Clustering beneath the long descent
   And grey slopes of the wold,
The red roofs nestle, oversprent
   With lichen yellow as gold.

We found it in the mid-day sun
   Basking, what time of year
The thrush his singing has begun
   Ere the first leaves appear.

High from his load a woodman pitched
   His faggots on the stack:
Knee-deep in straw the cattle twitched
   Sweet hay from crib and rack:

And from the barn hard by was borne
   A steady muffled din,
By which we knew that threshèd corn
   Was winnowing, and went in.

The sunbeams on the motey air
   Streamed through the open door,
And on the brown arms moving bare,
   And the grain upon the floor.

One turns the crank, one stoops to feed
   The hopper, lest it lack,
One in the bushel scoops the seed,
   One stands to hold the sack.

We watched the good grain rattle down,
   And the awns fly in the draught;
To see us both so pensive grown
   The honest labourers laughed:

Merry they were, because the wheat
   Was clean and plump and good,
Pleasant to hand and eye, and meet
   For market and for food.

It chanced we from the city were,
   And had not gat us free
In spirit from the store and stir
   Of its immensity:

But here we found ourselves again.
   Where humble harvests bring
After much toil but little grain,
   'Tis merry winnowing.

'The birds that sing on autumn eves'

The birds that sing on autumn eves
Among the golden-tinted leaves,
Are but the few that true remain
Of budding May's rejoicing train.

Like autumn flowers that brave the frost,
And make their show when hope is lost,
These 'mong the fruits and mellow scent
Mourn not the high-sunned summer spent.

Their notes thro' all the jocund spring
Were mixed in merry musicking:
They sang for love the whole day long,
But now their love is all for song.

Now each hath perfected his lay
To praise the year that hastes away:
They sit on boughs apart, and vie
In single songs and rich reply:

And oft as in the copse I hear
These anthems of the dying year,
The passions, once her peace that stole,
With flattering love my heart console.

The Garden in September

Now thin mists temper the slow-ripening beams
Of the September sun: his golden gleams
On gaudy flowers shine, that prank the rows
Of high-grown hollyhocks, and all tall shows
That Autumn flaunteth in his bushy bowers;
Where tomtits, hanging from the drooping heads
Of giant sunflowers, peck the nutty seeds;
And in the feathery aster bees on wing
Seize and set free the honied flowers,
Till thousand stars leap with their visiting:
While ever across the path mazily flit,
Unpiloted in the sun,
The dreamy butterflies
With dazzling colours powdered and soft glooms,
White, black and crimson stripes, and peacock eyes,
Or on chance flowers sit,
With idle effort plundering one by one
The nectaries of deepest-throated blooms.

With gentle flaws the western breeze
Into the garden saileth,
Scarce here and there stirring the single trees,
For his sharpness he vaileth:
So long a comrade of the bearded corn,
Now from the stubbles whence the shocks are borne,
O'er dewy lawns he turns to stray,
As mindful of the kisses and soft play
Wherewith he enamoured the light-hearted May,
Ere he deserted her;

Lover of fragrance, and too late repents;
Nor more of heavy hyacinth now may drink,
Nor spicy pink,
Nor summer's rose, nor garnered lavender,
But the few lingering scents
Of streakèd pea, and gillyflower, and stocks
Of courtly purple, and aromatic phlox.

And at all times to hear are drowsy tones
Of dizzy flies, and humming drones,
With sudden flap of pigeon wings in the sky,
Or the wild cry
Of thirsty rooks, that scour ascare
The distant blue, to watering as they fare
With creaking pinions, or – on business bent,
If aught their ancient polity displease, –
Come gathering to their colony, and there
Settling in ragged parliament,
Some stormy council hold in the high trees.

North Wind in October

In the golden glade the chestnuts are fallen all;
From the sered boughs of the oak the acorns fall:
The beech scatters her ruddy fire;
The lime hath stripped to the cold,
And standeth naked above her yellow attire:
The larch thinneth her spire
To lay the ways of the wood with cloth of gold.

   Out of the golden-green and white
Of the brake the fir-trees stand upright
In the forest of flame, and wave aloft
To the blue of heaven their blue-green tuftings soft.

But swiftly in shuddering gloom the splendours fail,
As the harrying North-wind beareth
A cloud of skirmishing hail
The grievèd woodland to smite:
In a hurricane through the trees he teareth,
Raking the boughs and the leaves rending,
And whistleth to the descending
Blows of his icy flail.
Gold and snow he mixeth in spite,
And whirleth afar; as away on his winnowing flight
He passeth, and all again for awhile is bright.

November

The lonely season in lonely lands, when fled
Are half the birds, and mists lie low, and the sun
Is rarely seen, nor strayeth far from his bed;
The short days pass unwelcomed one by one.

   Out by the ricks the mantled engine stands
Crestfallen, deserted, – for now all hands
Are told to the plough, – and ere it is dawn appear
The teams following and crossing far and near,
As hour by hour they broaden the brown bands
Of the striped fields; and behind them firk and prance
The heavy rooks, and daws grey-pated dance:
As awhile, surmounting a crest, in sharp outline
(A miniature of toil, a gem's design,)
They are pictured, horses and men, or now near by
Above the lane they shout lifting the share,
By the trim hedgerow bloom'd with purple air;
Where, under the thorns, dead leaves in huddle lie
Packed by the gales of Autumn, and in and out
The small wrens glide
With a happy note of cheer,
And yellow amorets flutter above and about,
Gay, familiar in fear.

   And now, if the night shall be cold, across the sky
Linnets and twites, in small flocks helter-skelter,
All the afternoon to the gardens fly,
From thistle-pastures hurrying to gain the shelter
Of American rhododendron or cherry-laurel:
And here and there, near chilly setting of sun,

In an isolated tree a congregation
Of starlings chatter and chide,
Thickset as summer leaves, in garrulous quarrel:
Suddenly they hush as one, –
The tree top springs, –
And off, with a whirr of wings,
They fly by the score
To the holly-thicket, and there with myriads more
Dispute for the roosts; and from the unseen nation
A babel of tongues, like running water unceasing,
Makes live the wood, the flocking cries increasing,
Wrangling discordantly, incessantly,
While falls the night on them self-occupied;
The long dark night, that lengthens slow,
Deepening with Winter to starve grass and tree,
And soon to bury in snow
The Earth, that, sleeping 'neath her frozen stole,
Shall dream a dream crept from the sunless pole
Of how her end shall be.

The South Wind

The south wind rose at dusk of the winter day,
The warm breath of the western sea
Circling wrapp'd the isle with his cloke of cloud,
And it now reach'd even to me, at dusk of the day,
And moan'd in the branches aloud:
While here and there, in patches of dark space,
A star shone forth from its heavenly place,
As a spark that is borne in the smoky chase;
And, looking up, there fell on my face –
Could it be drops of rain
Soft as the wind, that fell on my face?
Gossamers light as threads of the summer dawn,
Suck'd by the sun from midmost calms of the main,
From groves of coral islands secretly drawn,
O'er half the round of earth to be driven,
Now to fall on my face
In silky skeins spun from the mists of heaven.

Who art thou, in wind and darkness and soft rain
Thyself that robest, that bendest in sighing pines
To whisper thy truth? that usest for signs
A hurried glimpse of the moon, the glance of a star
In the rifted sky?
Who art thou, that with thee I
Woo and am wooed?
That robing thyself in darkness and soft rain
Choosest my chosen solitude,
Coming so far
To tell thy secret again,
As a mother her child, in her folding arm
Of a winter night by a flickering fire,
Telleth the same tale o'er and o'er
With gentle voice, and I never tire,
So imperceptibly changeth the charm,
As Love on buried ecstasy buildeth his tower,
– Like as the stem that beareth the flower
By trembling is knit to power; –
Ah! long ago
In thy first rapture I renounced my lot,
The vanity, the despondency and the woe,
And seeking thee to know
Well was't for me, and evermore
I am thine, I know not what.

For me thou seekest ever, me wondering a day
In the eternal alternations, me
Free for a stolen moment of chance
To dream a beautiful dream
In the everlasting dance
Of speechless worlds, the unsearchable scheme,
To me thou findest the way,
Me and whomsoe'er
I have found my dream to share
Still with thy charm encircling; even to-night
To me and my love in darkness and soft rain
Under the sighing pines thou comest again,
And staying our speech with mystery of delight,
Of the kiss that I give a wonder thou makest,
And the kiss that I take thou takest.

London Snow

When men were all asleep the snow came flying,
In large white flakes falling on the city brown,
Stealthily and perpetually settling and loosely lying,
    Hushing the latest traffic of the drowsy town;
Deadening, muffling, stifling its murmurs failing;
Lazily and incessantly floating down and down:
    Silently sifting and veiling road, roof and railing;
Hiding difference, making unevenness even,
Into angles and crevices softly drifting and sailing.
    All night it fell, and when full inches seven
It lay in the depth of its uncompacted lightness,
The clouds blew off from a high and frosty heaven;
    And all woke earlier for the unaccustomed brightness
Of the winter dawning, the strange unheavenly glare:
The eye marvelled – marvelled at the dazzling whiteness;
    The ear hearkened to the stillness of the solemn air;
No sound of wheel rumbling nor of foot falling,
And the busy morning cries came thin and spare.
    Then boys I heard, as they went to school, calling,
They gathered up the crystal manna to freeze
Their tongues with tasting, their hands with snowballing;
    Or rioted in a drift, plunging up to the knees;
Or peering up from under the white-mossed wonder,
'O look at the trees!' they cried, 'O look at the trees!'
    With lessened load a few carts creak and blunder,
Following along the white deserted way,
A country company long dispersed asunder:
    When now already the sun, in pale display
Standing by Paul's high dome, spread forth below
His sparkling beams, and awoke the stir of the day.

For now doors open, and war is waged with the snow;
And trains of sombre men, past tale of number,
Tread long brown paths, as toward their toil they go:
　　But even for them awhile no cares encumber
Their minds diverted; the daily word is unspoken,
The daily thoughts of labour and sorrow slumber
At the sight of the beauty that greets them, for the charm they
　　have broken.

Winter Nightfall

The day begins to droop, –
    Its course is done:
But nothing tells the place
    Of the setting sun.

The hazy darkness deepens,
    And up the lane
You may hear, but cannot see,
    The homing wain.

An engine pants and hums
    In the farm hard by:
Its lowering smoke is lost
    In the lowering sky.

The soaking branches drip,
    And all night through
The dropping will not cease
    In the avenue.

A tall man there in the house
    Must keep his chair:
He knows he will never again
    Breathe the spring air:

His heart is worn with work;
    He is giddy and sick
If he rise to go as far
    As the nearest rick:

He thinks of his morn of life,
    His hale, strong years;
And braves as he may the night
    Of darkness and tears.

Love Poems

'Awake, my heart, to be loved, awake, awake!'

Awake, my heart, to be loved, awake, awake!
The darkness silvers away, the morn doth break,
It leaps in the sky: unrisen lustres slake
The o'ertaken moon. Awake, O heart, awake!

She too that loveth awaketh and hopes for thee;
Her eyes already have sped the shades that flee,
Already they watch the path thy feet shall take:
Awake, O heart, to be loved, awake, awake!

And if thou tarry from her, – if this could be, –
She cometh herself, O heart, to be loved, to thee;
For thee would unashamèd herself forsake:
Awake to be loved, my heart, awake, awake!

Awake, the land is scattered with light, and see,
Uncanopied sleep is flying from field and tree:
And blossoming boughs of April in laughter shake;
Awake, O heart, to be loved, awake, awake!

Lo all things wake and tarry and look for thee:
She looketh and saith, 'O sun, now bring him to me.
Come more adored, O adored, for his coming's sake,
And awake my heart to be loved: awake, awake!'

'Love on my heart from heaven fell'

Love on my heart from heaven fell,
Soft as the dew on flowers of spring,
Sweet as the hidden drops that swell
Their honey-throated chalicing.

Now never from him do I part,
Hosanna evermore I cry:
I taste his savour in my heart,
And bid all praise him as do I.

Without him noughtsoever is,
Nor was afore, nor e'er shall be:
Nor any other joy than his
Wish I for mine to comfort me.

'The evening darkens over'

The evening darkens over
After a day so bright
The windcapt waves discover
That wild will be the night.
There's sound of distant thunder.

The latest sea-birds hover
Along the cliff's sheer height;
As in the memory wander
Last flutterings of delight,
White wings lost on the white.

There's not a ship in sight;
And as the sun goes under
Thick clouds conspire to cover
The moon that should rise yonder.
Thou art alone, fond lover.

'To my love I whisper, and say'

To my love I whisper, and say
Knowest thou why I love thee? – Nay:
Nay, she saith; O tell me again. –

When in her ear the secret I tell,
She smileth with joy incredible –

Ha! she is vain – O nay –
Then tell us! Nay, O nay.

But this is in my heart,
That Love is Nature's perfect art,
And man hath got his fancy hence,
To clothe his thought in forms of sense.

Fair are thy works, O man, and fair
Thy dreams of soul in garments rare,
Beautiful past compare,
Yea, godlike when thou hast the skill
To steal a stir of the heavenly thrill:

But O, have care, have care!
'Tis envious even to dare:
And many a fiend is watching well
To flush thy reed with the fire of hell.

Song

I love my lady's eyes
Above the beauties rare
She most is wont to prize,
Above her sunny hair,
And all that face to face
Her glass repeats of grace.

For those are still the same
To her and all that see:
But oh! her eyes will flame
When they do look on me:
And so above the rest
I love her eyes the best.

Now say, (*Say, O say! saith the music*)
    who likes my song? –
I knew you by your eyes,
That rest on nothing long,
And have forgot surprise;
And stray (*Stray, O stray! saith the music*)
    as mine will stray,
The while my love's away.

'My spirit kisseth thine'

My spirit kisseth thine,
My spirit embraceth thee:
I feel thy being twine
Her graces over me,

   In the life-kindling fold
Of God's breath; where on high,
In furthest space untold
Like a lost world I lie:

   And o'er my dreaming plains
Lightens, most pale and fair,
A moon that never wanes;
Or more, if I compare,

   Like what the shepherd sees
On late mid-winter dawns,
When thro' the branchèd trees,
O'er the white-frosted lawns,

   The huge unclouded sun,
Surprising the world whist,
Is all uprisen thereon,
Golden with melting mist.

'My delight and thy delight'

My delight and thy delight
Walking, like two angels white,
In the gardens of the night:

My desire and thy desire
Twining to a tongue of fire,
Leaping live, and laughing higher;
Thro' the everlasting strife
In the mystery of life.

Love, from whom the world begun,
Hath the secret of the sun.

Love can tell, and love alone,
Whence the million stars were strewn,
Why each atom knows its own,
How, in spite of woe and death,
Gay is life, and sweet is breath:

This he taught us, this we knew,
Happy in his science true,
Hand in hand as we stood
Neath the shadows of the wood,
Heart to heart as we lay
In the dawning of the day.

Anniversary

What is sweeter than new-mown hay,
Fresher than winds o'er-sea that blow,
Innocent above children's play,
Fairer and purer than winter snow,
Frolic as are the morns of May?
– If it should be what best I know!

What is richer than thoughts that stray
From reading of poems that smoothly flow?
What is solemn like the delay
Of concords linked in a music slow
Dying thro' vaulted aisles away?
– If it should be what best I know!

What gives faith to me when I pray,
Setteth my heart with joy aglow,
Filleth my song with fancies gay,
Maketh the heaven to which I go,
The gladness of earth that lasteth for aye?
– If it should be what best I know!

But tell me thou – 'twas on this day
That first we loved five years ago –
If 'tis a thing that I can say,
   Though it must be what best we know.

'So sweet love seemed that April morn'

So sweet love seemed that April morn,
When first we kissed beside the thorn,
So strangely sweet, it was not strange
We thought that love could never change.

But I can tell – let truth be told –
That love will change in growing old;
Though day by day is nought to see,
So delicate his motions be.

And in the end 'twill come to pass
Quite to forget what once he was,
Nor even in fancy to recall
The pleasure that was all in all.

His little spring, that sweet we found,
So deep in summer floods is drowned,
I wonder, bathed in joy complete,
How love so young could be so sweet.

The Philosopher to his Mistress

Because thou canst not see,
Because thou canst not know
The black and hopeless woe
That hath encompassed me:
Because, should I confess
The thought of my despair,
My words would wound thee less
Than swords can hurt the air:

Because with thee I seem
As one invited near
To taste the faery cheer
Of spirits in a dream;
Of whom he knoweth nought
Save that they vie to make
All motion, voice and thought
A pleasure for his sake:

Therefore more sweet and strange
Has been the mystery
Of thy long love to me,
That doth not quit, nor change,
Nor tax my solemn heart,
That kisseth in a gloom,
Knowing not who thou art
That givest, nor to whom.

Therefore the tender touch
Is more; more dear the smile:
And thy light words beguile
My wisdom overmuch:
And O with swiftness fly
The fancies of my song
To happy worlds, where I
Still in thy love belong.

'Thou didst delight my eyes'

Thou didst delight my eyes:
Yet who am I? nor first
Nor last nor best, that durst
Once dream of thee for prize;
Nor this the only time
Thou shalt set love to rhyme.

Thou didst delight my ear:
Ah! little praise; thy voice
Makes other hearts rejoice,
Makes all ears glad that hear;
And short my joy: but yet,
O song, do not forget!

For what wert thou to me?
How shall I say? The moon,
That poured her midnight noon
Upon his wrecking sea; –
A sail, that for a day
Has cheered the castaway.

Vivamus

When thou didst give thy love to me,
　　Asking no more of gods or men
I vow'd I would contented be,
　　If Fate should grant us summers ten.

But now that twice the term is sped,
　　And ever young my heart and gay,
I fear the words that then I said,
　　And turn my face from Fate away.

To bid thee happily good-bye
　　I have no hope that I can see,
No way that I shall bravely die,
　　Unless I give my life for thee.

                                    1901

'Since to be loved endures'

Since to be loved endures,
　　To love is wise:
Earth hath no good but yours,
　　Brave, joyful eyes:

Earth hath no sin but thine,
　　Dull eye of scorn:
O'er thee the sun doth pine
　　And angels mourn.

Eros

Why hast thou nothing in thy face?
Thou idol of the human race,
Thou tyrant of the human heart,
The flower of lovely youth that art;
Yea, and that standest in thy youth
An image of eternal Truth,
With thy exuberant flesh so fair,
That only Pheidias might compare,
Ere from his chaste marmoreal form
Time had decayed the colours warm;
Like to his gods in thy proud dress,
Thy starry sheen of nakedness.

Surely thy body is thy mind,
For in thy face is nought to find,
Only thy soft unchristen'd smile,
That shadows neither love nor guile,
But shameless will and power immense,
In secret sensuous innocence.

O king of joy, what is thy thought?
I dream thou knowest it is nought,
And wouldst in darkness come, but thou
Makest the light where'er thou go.
Ah yet no victim of thy grace,
None who e'er long'd for thy embrace,
Hath cared to look upon thy face.

'Will Love again awake'

MUSE

Will Love again awake,
That lies asleep so long?

POET

O hush! ye tongues that shake
The drowsy night with song

MUSE

It is a lady fair
Whom once he deigned to praise,
That at the door doth dare
Her sad complaint to raise.

POET

She must be fair of face,
As bold of heart she seems,
If she would match her grace
With the delight of dreams.

MUSE

Her beauty would surprise
Gazers on Autumn eves,
Who watched the broad moon rise
Upon the scattered sheaves.

POET

O sweet must be the voice
He shall descend to hear,
Who doth in Heaven rejoice
His most enchanted ear.

MUSE

The smile, that rests to play
Upon her lip, foretells
What musical array
Tricks her sweet syllables.

POET

And yet her smiles have danced
In vain, if her discourse
Win not the soul entranced
In divine intercourse.

MUSE

She will encounter all
This trial without shame,
Her eyes men Beauty call,
And Wisdom is her name.

POET

Throw back the portals then,
Ye guards, your watch that keep,
Love will awake again
That lay so long asleep.

Miscellaneous

'Angel spirits of sleep'

Angel spirits of sleep,
White-robed, with silver hair;
In your meadows fair,
Where the willows weep,
And the sad moonbeam
On the gliding stream
Writes her scattered dream:

Angel spirits of sleep,
Dancing to the weir
In the hollow roar
Of its waters deep;
Know ye how men say
That ye haunt no more
Isle and grassy shore
With your moonlit play;
That ye dance not here,
White-robed spirits of sleep,
All the summer night
Threading dances light?

A Passer-by

Whither, O splendid ship, thy white sails crowding,
  Leaning across the bosom of the urgent West,
That fearest nor sea rising, nor sky clouding,
  Whither away, fair rover, and what thy quest?
  Ah! soon, when Winter has all our vales opprest,
When skies are cold and misty, and hail is hurling,
  Wilt thóu glíde on the blue Pacific, or rest
In a summer haven asleep, thy white sails furling.

I there before thee, in the country that well thou knowest,
  Already arrived am inhaling the odorous air:
I watch thee enter unerringly where thou goest,
  And anchor queen of the strange shipping there,
  Thy sails for awnings spread, thy masts bare;
Nor is aught from the foaming reef to the snow-capped, grandest
  Peak, that is over the feathery palms more fair
Than thou, so upright, so stately, and still thou standest.

And yet, O splendid ship, unhailed and nameless,
  I know not if, aiming a fancy, I rightly divine
That thou hast a purpose joyful, a courage blameless,
  Thy port assured in a happier land than mine.
But for all I have given thee, beauty enough is thine,
As thou, aslant with trim tackle and shrouding,
  From the proud nostril curve of a prow's line
In the offing scatterest foam, thy white sails crowding.

Noel: Christmas Eve, 1913

Pax hominibus benae voluntatis

A frosty Christmas Eve
   when the stars were shining
Fared I forth alone
   where westward falls the hill,
And from many a village
   in the water'd valley
Distant music reach'd me
   peals of bells aringing:
The constellated sounds
   ran sprinkling on earth's floor
As the dark vault above
   with stars was spangled o'er.

Then sped my thought to keep
   that first Christmas of all
When the shepherds watching
   by their folds ere the dawn
Heard music in the fields
   and marveling could not tell
Whether it were angels
   or the bright stars singing.

Now blessed be the tow'rs
   that crown England so fair
That stand up strong in prayer
   unto God for our souls:
Blessed be their founders
   (said I) an' our country folk

Who are ringing for Christ
in the belfries to-night
With arms lifted to clutch
the rattling ropes that race
Into the dark above
and the mad romping din.

But to me heard afar
it was starry music
Angels' song, comforting
as the comfort of Christ
When he spake tenderly
to his sorrowful flock:
The old words came to me
by the riches of time
Mellow'd and transfigured
as I stood on the hill
Heark'ning in the aspect
of th' eternal silence.

Low Barometer

The south-wind strengthens to a gale,
Across the moon the clouds fly fast,
The house is smitten as with a flail,
The chimney shudders to the blast.

On such a night, when Air has loosed
Its guardian grasp on blood and brain,
Old terrors then of god or ghost
Creep from their caves to life again;

And Reason kens he herits in
A haunted house. Tenants unknown
Assert their squalid lease of sin
With earlier title than his own.

Unbodied presences, the pack'd
Pollution and remorse of Time,
Slipp'd from oblivion reënact
The horrors of unhouseld crime.

Some men would quell the thing with prayer
Whose sightless footsteps pad the floor,
Whose fearful trespass mounts the stair
Or bursts the lock'd forbidden door.

Some have seen corpses long interr'd
Escape from hallowing control,
Pale charnel forms – nay ev'n have heard
The shrilling of a troubled soul,

That wanders till the dawn hath cross'd
The dolorous dark, or Earth hath wound
Closer her storm-spredd cloke, and thrust
The baleful phantoms underground.

'I heard great Hector
sounding war's alarms'

I heard great Hector sounding war's alarms,
Where thro' the listless ghosts chiding he strode,
As tho' the Greeks besieged his last abode,
And he his Troy's hope still, her king-at-arms.
But on those gentle meads, which Lethe charms
With weary oblivion, his passion glow'd
Like the cold night-worm's candle, and only show'd
Such mimic flame as neither heats nor harms.

   'Twas plain to read, even by those shadows quaint,
How rude catastrophe had dim'd his day,
And blighted all his cheer with stern complaint:
To arms! to arms! what more the voice would say
Was swallow'd in the valleys, and grew faint
Upon the thin air, as he pass'd away.

Elegy

ON A LADY, WHOM GRIEF FOR
THE DEATH OF HER BETROTHED KILLED

Assemble, all ye maidens, at the door,
And all ye loves, assemble; far and wide
Proclaim the bridal, that proclaimed before
Has been deferred to this late eventide:
      For on this night the bride,
    The days of her betrothal over,
  Leaves the parental hearth for evermore;
To-night the bride goes forth to meet her lover.

Reach down the wedding vesture, that has lain
    Yet all unvisited, the silken gown:
Bring out the bracelets, and the golden chain
  Her dearer friends provided: sere and brown
      Bring out the festal crown,
    And set it on her forehead lightly:
  Though it be withered, twine no wreath again;
This only is the crown she can wear rightly.

Cloke her in ermine, for the night is cold,
And wrap her warmly, for the night is long,
In pious hands the flaming torches hold,
While her attendants, chosen from among
      Her faithful virgin throng,
    May lay her in her cedar litter,
  Decking her coverlet with sprigs of gold,
Roses, and lilies white that best befit her.

Sound flute and tabor, that the bridal be
Not without music, nor with these alone;
But let the viol lead the melody,
With lesser intervals, and plaintive moan
        Of sinking semitone;
    And, all in choir, the virgin voices
  Rest not from singing in skilled harmony
The song that aye the bridegroom's ear rejoices.

Let the priests go before, arrayed in white,
And let the dark-stoled minstrels follow slow,
Next they that bear her, honoured on this night,
And then the maidens, in a double row,
        Each singing soft and low,
    And each on high a torch upstaying:
  Unto her lover lead her forth with light,
With music, and with singing, and with praying.

'Twas at this sheltering hour he nightly came,
And found her trusty window open wide,
And knew the signal of the timorous flame,
That long the restless curtain would not hide
        Her form that stood beside;
    As scarce she dared to be delighted,
  Listening to that sweet tale, that is no shame
To faithful lovers, that their hearts have plighted.

But now for many days the dewy grass
Has shown no markings of his feet at morn:
And watching she has seen no shadow pass
The moonlit walk, and heard no music borne
        Upon her ear forlorn.
    In vain has she looked out to greet him;

He has not come, he will not come, alas!
So let us bear her out where she must meet him.

Now to the river bank the priests are come:
The bark is ready to receive its freight:
Let some prepare her place therein, and some
Embark the litter with its slender weight:
　　The rest stand by in state,
　　And sing her a safe passage over;
　While she is oared across to her new home,
Into the arms of her expectant lover.

And thou, O lover, that art on the watch,
Where, on the banks of the forgetful streams,
The pale indifferent ghosts wander, and snatch
The sweeter moments of their broken dreams, –
　　Thou, when the torchlight gleams,
　　When thou shalt see the slow procession,
　And when thine ears the fitful music catch,
Rejoice, for thou art near to thy possession.

The Testament of Beauty

Bridges's last and most original work was a long philosophic poem, 'The Testament of Beauty'. Always a technical experimentalist, he devised for it a new metre, described by him as 'rhymeless, loose, alexandrines', intended to be flexible enough easily to express intellectual discourse. Alas, poetry and philosophy are seldom happy companions to one another; nor did Bridges often manage to make them so. For the most part the loose alexandrines, sunk under the weight of philosophizing, remain obstinately unpoetical. But now and again in order to illustrate a point, the poet inserts characteristic passages of natural description or personal reflection. These display his art at its best, refreshed and invigorated by the new and freer form in which it shows itself.

from The Testament of Beauty

INTRODUCTION

. . . 'Twas late in my long journey, when I had clomb to where
the path was narrowing and the company few,
a glow of childlike wonder enthral'd me, as if my sense
had come to a new birth purified, my mind enrapt
re-awakening to a fresh initiation of life;
with like surprise of joy as any man may know
who rambling wide hath turn'd, resting on some hill-top
to view the plain he has left, and see'th it now out-spredd
mapp'd at his feet, a landscape so by beauty estranged
he scarce wil ken familiar haunts, nor his own home,
maybe, where far it lieth, small as a faded thought.
   Or as I well remember one highday in June
bright on the seaward South-downs, where I had come afar
on a wild garden planted years agone, and fenced
thickly within live-beechen walls: the season it was
of prodigal gay blossom, and man's skill had made
a fair-order'd husbandry of thatt nativ pleasaunce:
But had ther been no more than earth's wild loveliness,
the blue sky and soft air and the unmown flowersprent lawns,
I would hav lain me down and long'd, as then I did,
to lie there ever indolently undisturb'd, and watch
the common flowers that starr'd the fine grass of the wold,
waving in gay display their gold-heads to the sun,
each telling of its own inconscient happiness,
each type a faultless essence of God's will, such gems
as magic master-minds in painting or music
threw aside once for man's regard or disregard;
things supreme in themselves, eternal, unnumber'd
in the unexplored necessities of Life and Love.

[157]

To such a mood I had come, by what charm I know not,
where on thatt upland path I was pacing alone;
and yet was nothing new to me, only all was vivid
and significant that had been dormant or dead:
as if in a museum the fossils on their shelves
should come to life suddenly, or a winter rose-bed
burst into crowded holiday of scent and bloom.
I felt the domination of Nature's secret urge,
and happy escape therein; as when in boyhood once
from the rattling workshops of a great factory
conducted into the engine-room I stood in face
of the quiet driving power, that fast in nether cave
seated, set all the floors a-quiver, a thousand looms
throbbing and jennies dancing; and I felt at heart
a kinship with it and sympathy, as children wil
with amicable monsters: for in truth the mind
is indissociable from what it contemplates,
as thirst and generous wine are to a man that drinketh
nor kenneth whether his pleasur is more in his desire
or in the savor of the rich grape that allays it.

Man's Reason is in such deep insolvency to sense,
that tho' she guide his highest flight heav'nward, and teach
    him
dignity morals manners and human comfort,
she can delicately and dangerously bedizen
the rioting joys that fringe the sad pathways of Hell.
Nor without alliance of the animal senses
hath she any miracle: Lov'st thou in the blithe hour
of April dawns – nay marvelest thou not – to hear
the ravishing music that the small birdës make
in garden or woodland, rapturously heralding
the break of day; when the first lark on high hath warn'd

the vigilant robin already of the sun's approach,
and he on slender pipe calleth the nesting tribes
to awake and fill and thrill their myriad-warbling throats
praising life's God, untill the blisful revel grow
in wild profusion unfeign'd to such a hymn as man
hath never in temple or grove pour'd to the Lord of heav'n?

   Hast thou then thought that all this ravishing music,
that stirreth so thy heart, making thee dream of things
illimitable unsearchable and of heavenly import,
is but a light disturbance of the atoms of air,
whose jostling ripples, gather'd within the ear, are tuned
to resonant scale, and thence by the enthron'd mind received
on the spiral stairway of her audience chamber
as heralds of high spiritual significance?
and that without thine ear, sound would hav no report.
Nature hav no music; nor would ther be for thee
any better melody in the April woods at dawn
than what an old stone-deaf labourer, lying awake
o'night in his comfortless attic, might perchance
be aware of, when the rats run amok in his thatch?

* * *

Clouds and Trees
from Introduction

The sky's unresting cloudland, that with varying play
sifteth the sunlight thru' its figured shades, that now
stand in massiv range, cumulated stupendous
mountainous snowbillowy up-piled in dazzling sheen,
Now like sailing ships on a calm ocean drifting,

[159]

Now scatter'd wispy waifs, that neath the eager blaze
disperse in air; Or now parcelling the icy inane
highspredd in fine diaper of silver and mother-of-pearl
freaking the intense azure; Now scurrying close o'erhead,
wild ink-hued random racers that fling sheeted rain
gustily, and with garish bows laughing o'erarch the land:
Or, if the spirit of storm be abroad, huge molten glooms
mount on the horizon stealthily, and gathering as they climb
deep-freighted with live lightning, thunder and drenching
    flood
rebuff the winds, and with black-purpling terror impend
til they be driven away, when grave Night peacefully
clearing her heav'nly rondure of its turbid veils
layeth bare the playthings of Creation's babyhood;
and the immortal fireballs of her uttermost space
twinkle like friendly rushlights on the countryside.
    Them soon the jealous Day o'errideth to display
Earth's green robe, which the sun fostereth for shelter and
    shower
The dance of young trees that in a wild birch-spinney
toss to and fro the cluster of their flickering crests,
as rye curtseying in array to the breeze of May;
The ancestral trunks that mightily in the forest choirs
rear stedfast colonnade, or imperceptibly
    sway in tall pinewoods to their whispering spires;
The woodland's alternating hues, the vaporous bloom
of the first blushings and tender flushings of spring;
The slumbrous foliage of high midsummer's wealth;
Rich Autumn's golden quittance, to the bankruptcy
of the black shapely skeletons standing in snow:

Plough and Harvest
from Book III

How was November's melancholy endear'd to me
in the effigy of plowteams following and recrossing
patiently the desolat landscape from dawn to dusk,
as the slow-creeping ripple of their single furrow
submerged the sodden litter of summer's festival!
They are fled, those gracious teams; high on the headland now
squatted, a roaring engin toweth to itself
a beam of bolted shares, that glideth to and fro
combing the stubbled glebe: and agriculture here,
blotting out with such daub so rich a pictur of grace,
hath lost as much of beauty as it hath saved in toil.
   Again where reapers, bending to the ripen'd corn,
were wont to scythe in rank and step with measured stroke,
a shark-tooth'd chariot rampeth biting a broad way,
and, jerking its high swindging arms around in the air,
swoopeth the swath. Yet this queer Pterodactyl is well,
that in the sinister torpor of the blazing day
clicketeth in heartless mockery of swoon and sweat,
as 'twer the salamandrine voice of all parch'd things:
and the dry grasshopper wondering knoweth his God.
   Or what man feeleth not a new poetry of toil,
whenas on frosty evenings neath its clouding smoke
the engin hath huddled-up its clumsy threshing-coach
against the ricks, wherefrom laborers standing aloft
toss the sheaves on its tongue; while the grain runneth out,
and in the whirr of its multitudinous hurry
it hummeth like the bee, a warm industrious boom
that comforteth the farm, and spreadeth far afield
with throbbing power; as when in a cathedral awhile

the great diapason speaketh, and the painted saints
feel their glass canopies flutter in the heav'nward prayer.

Garden Scents
from Book IV

. . . The imponderable fragrance
of my window-jasmin, that from her starry cup
of red-stemm'd ivory invadeth my being,
as she floateth it forth, and wantoning unabash'd
asserteth her idea in the omnipotent blaze
of the tormented sun-ball, checquering the grey wall
with shadow-tracery of her shapely fronds; this frail
unique spice of perfumery, in which she holdeth
monopoly by royal licence of Nature,
is but one of a thousand angelic species,
original beauties that win conscience in man:
a like marvel hangeth o'er the rosebed, and where
the honeysuckle escapeth in serpentine sprays
from its dark-cloister'd clamber thru' the old holly-bush,
spreading its joybunches to finger at the sky
in revel above rivalry. Legion is their name;
Lily-of-the-vale, Violet, Verbena, Mignonette,
Hyacinth, Heliotrope, Sweet-briar, Pinks and Peas,
Lilac and Wallflower, or such white and purple blooms
that sleep i' the sun, and their heavy perfumes withhold
to mingle their heart's incense with the wonder-dreams,
love-laden prayers and reveries that steal forth from earth,
under the dome of night: and tho' these blossomy breaths,
that hav presumed the title of their gay genitors,
enter but singly into our neighboring sense, that hath

no panorama, yet the mind's eye is not blind
unto their multitudinous presences: – I know
that if odour wer visible as color is, I'd see
the summer garden aureoled in rainbow clouds,
with such warfare of hues as a painter might choose
to show his sunset sky or a forest aflame;
while o'er the country-side the wide clover-pastures
and the beanfields of June would wear a mantle, thick
as when in late October, at the drooping of day
the dark grey mist arising blotteth out the land
with ghostly shroud . . .

Farewell
from Book IV

'Twas at thatt hour of beauty when the setting sun
squandereth his cloudy bed with rosy hues, to flood
his lov'd works as in turn he biddeth them Good-night;
and all the towers and temples and mansions of men
face him in bright farewell, ere they creep from their pomp
naked beneath the darkness; – while to mortal eyes
'tis given, if so they close not of fatigue, nor strain
at lamplit tasks – 'tis given, as for a royal boon
to beggarly outcasts in homeless vigil, to watch
where uncurtain'd behind the great windows of space
Heav'n's jewel'd company circleth unapproachably –
'Twas at sunset that I, fleeing to hide my soul
in refuge of beauty from a mortal distress,
walk'd alone with the Muse in her garden of thought,
discoursing at liberty with the mazy dreams
that came wavering pertinaciously about me; as when

the small bats, issued from their hangings, flitter o'erhead
thru' the summer twilight, with thin cries to and fro
hunting in muffled flight atween the stars and flowers.

Then fell I in strange delusion, illusion strange to tell;
for as a man who lyeth fast asleep in his bed
may dream he waketh, and that he walketh upright
pursuing some endeavour in full conscience – so 'twas
with me; but contrawise; for being in truth awake
methought I slept and dreamt; and in thatt dream methought
I was telling a dream; nor telling was I as one
who, truly awaked from a true sleep, thinketh to tell
his dream to a friend, but for his scant remembrances
findeth no token of speech – it was not so with me;
for my tale was my dream and my dream the telling,
and I remember wondring the while I told it
how I told it so tellingly. And yet now 'twould seem
that Reason inveigled me with her old orderings;
as once when she took thought to adjust theology,
peopling the inane that vex'd her between God and man
with a hierarchy of angels; like those asteroids
wherewith she later fill'd the gap 'twixt Jove and Mars.

Verily by Beauty it is that we come at WISDOM,
yet not by Reason at Beauty: and now with many words
pleasing myself betimes I am fearing lest in the end
I play the tedious orator who maundereth on
for lack of heart to make an end of his nothings.
Wherefor as when a runner who hath run his round
handeth his staff away, and is glad of his rest,
here break I off, knowing the goal was not for me
the while I ran on telling of what cannot be told . . .

Index of Titles and First Lines